CW00954460

1st edition February 2020
© 2020 edulink GmbH, Schubertstr. 12, 80336 Munich
Copyright reserved

Printing and binding: Amazon Media EU S.à r.l., 5 Rue Plaetis, L-2338, Luxembourg

ISBN 9798614645250

Your opinion is important to us! Suggestions, praise or criticism: info@edu-link.de

The Practice Test for the TestAS – Core Test
and Humanities, Cultural Studies
and Social Sciences

Özveri Bauschmid

WE ARE ASKING FOR YOUR HELP!

In order to keep our preparation books up to date and to ensure the best possible preparation for the St. Gallen admission test, we would like to ask for your help. If you have suggestions for improvement, for example if you have new questions types that we have not listed in our books or other information for more efficient preparation, please send us your feedback with the subject "FEEDBACK" to info@edu-link.de. We really appreciate your support. Please note our data protection regulations and legal information on page 197.

As a thank you, we give out an Amazon voucher worth €25 each month for the most helpful feedback. This promotion runs from Feb. 2020 to Jan. 2021. The deadline is the last day of the month.

Thank you very much!
Your edulink team

PREFACE

Attending university in Germany is an appealing option for many students from outside of the European Union. Germany has countless universities, many of which are recognized on an international level for their excellence. According to the 2019 Times World University Ranking, 35 of the world's 300 best universities are in Germany. As such, a Bachelor's or Master's degree from Germany can open the door to a variety of exciting career opportunities, both within Germany and worldwide. The multitude of programs offered in English, as well as the numerous funding options for international students (e.g. ERAMUS), make studying in Germany feasible for students from abroad. What's more, studying in Germany is also quite affordable: Since 2013, most universities have had no tuition fees for non-EU citizens (with the exception of universities in a few regions, such as Baden-Württemberg). Therefore, it is no surprise that an ever-rising number of non-EU applicants seek admission to German universities. As a result, the application pool is more for competitive than ever, and German universities have raised the difficulty of their admissions criteria for non-EU applicants. But do not despair. The fact that you are reading this book suggests that you are already on track to becoming a more competitive applicant.

There are certain things applicants can do to increase their chance of admission into German university. One is taking the Test for Foreign Students (TestAS). Over the years, the benefit of preparing for and taking this exam has become clear: applicants with competitive scores have are more likely to get accepted into to certain German universities. A good score can set you apart from other applicants, especially if you are applying to a program related to science, economics, or medicine.

The TestAS is a standardized exam for high-school graduates from countries outside of the European Union who hope to study at a German University. The test is offered by the Society for Academic Study Preparation and Test Development and is optional to applicants. The TestAS aims to measure cognitive and intellectual capabilities and has been used since 2007 as an aid to the application process to German universities. The test may be taken in German, English, and, in some cases, Arabic.

Competitive scores on the TestAS put applicants at an advantage when applying to certain universities. Participating universities use TestAS scores to evaluate the academic aptitude of potential students. As such, a good test score can greatly increase an applicant's chances of being admitted to his/her desired university and course of study. Good scores are also indicative that a student is likely to succeed in his/ her studies.

The TestAS consists of two sections: the core test and a subject module. The core test consists of four subsections and tests general cognitive skills. Every test taker completes the core test. We offer three preparation books for the core test to help you to master this test section. In contrast to the core test, test takers choose which specialist module to take. There are four options: mathematics and natural sciences, engineering, economics or the humanities. Applicants should select the subsection most relevant to the degree for which they are applying. The subsection aims to evaluate their aptitude within these specialized areas.

This book is a practice test, intended to help you prepare for test day by exposing you to the test format, question types, and time constraints. You will find a complete practice test with solutions and detailed explanations for each question of the core test and specialized modules "Humanities, Cultural and Social Sciences".

On our homepage www.testasprep.com you can also access our TestAS prep-books as ebooks, available in German and English, as well as lots of useful information about the exam. Our books are also available in print from Amazon.

We wish you success in your preparations and with the exam!

Best regards,
Your edulink team

TABLE OF CONTENTS

INTRODUCTION TO THE PRACTICE TEST

BENEFITS OF A PRACTICE TEST

Dear readers,

A practice test allows test-takers to experience the test format (test content as well as testing procedure) as they will on test day. This is crucial to identifying your specific test-taking weaknesses and developing effective preparation. Familiarizing yourself with the test format will help you arrive confident and well prepared for the exam.

The practice test gives you the opportunity to take the exam under real conditions. You will get to know the procedure of the exam, practice the variety of question types, experience the pressure of the time limits, and overall gain a good impression of what to expect. Through practice test you can determine how difficult it might be to concentrate for so many hours and you also get a good idea of how to pace yourself and manage time both within sections and while solving individual questions.

We advise you to take the practice test **in a single session**. Allow enough time to analyze your test results after the practice test. Doing this, you will address any gaps in your knowledge and achieve a better result on the test day. The test questions have been carefully selected and are based on extensive research and experience. In order to best simulate the exam situation, the questions also have varying levels of difficulty.

This practice test was designed to complement our series of TestAS preparation books. Our books for the Core Test as well both books for the section Humanities, Cultural Studies and Social Sciences are available for a more comprehensive treatment of the topics covered in the exam. In these books, we give you recommendations for answer strategies for various types of questions, in-depth explanations of common test topics that have been regularly asked in previous tests, as well as many exercise questions with detailed answers. We recommend that you first prepare with the preparation books and then practice with the practice test.

We hope that the following test will give you a comprehensive overview of what knowledge is expected of you enable you to develop familiarity with the question types of the admission test.

We wish you good luck!

STRUCTURE OF THE TEST

The test consists of seven subtests, that are made up by the Core Test and a subject-specific test module (Humanities-, Cultural Studies and Social Sciences).

The Core Test consists of four subtests:

- Solving Quantitative Problems
- Inferring Relationships
- Completing Patterns
- Continuing Numerical Series

The test module consists of three subtests:

- Understanding and Interpreting Texts
- Using Representations Systems Flexibly
- Recognizing Linguistic Structures

Exam sections and temporal sequence:

Section	Subtest	Number of tasks	Duration	Time per task
Core Test	Solving Quantitative Problems	22	45 min	~2 min
	Inferring Relationships	22	10 min	27 sec
	Completing Patterns	22	5 min reading- & 20 min working time	55 sec
	Continuing Numerical Series	22	5 min reading- & 25 min working time	68 sec
Break			~30 – 60 min	
Test Module	Understanding and Interpreting Texts	22	45 min	~2 sec
	Using Representation Systems Flexibly	22	55 min	2 min 50 sec
	Recognizing Linguistic Structures	22	50 min	2 min 27 sec
TOTAL			>5 hours	

Each subtest begins with an explanation and a sample question. The tasks of each subtest may be edited in any order. Choose one correct answer and mark it on your answer sheet.

Only the answers marked on the answer sheet will be graded.

TIPS ON TAKING THE PRACTICE TEST

For the following practice test, we highly recommend taking the test under real test conditions so that you experience your ability to work under time pressure for numerous hours. We recommend keeping track of time using a clock or stopwatch, and taking the test in one sitting, with a 30-minute break between core test and the subject module.

Replicating test conditions will allow you to notice when you run out of energy, and help determine how much food and drinks you should take with you on the day of the exam, since many test centers do not permit leaving the test grounds.

How to take the following test

1. Please cut out the blank answer sheets, which you can find in the appendix on the last pages of this test book.

2. Use a stop watch.

3. You don't get extra time to transfer your answers to the answer sheet. Only answers that are marked on the answer sheet will be counted. Please use a blue or black ballpoint pen for editing.

4. Note that there is only one correct answer for each question. If you mark more than one answer, the answer will be counted as wrong. In this case, you will not receive any points, even if one of the Xs was placed for the correct answer. Therefore, make sure that you only mark one answer at a time.

5. If the answer is incorrect, the question is given 0 points. This means, no points will be deducted, meaning there is no penalty for wrong answers. You should always guess.

6. During the test there is only a break after the first three sections. If you need additional breaks, know that the test timer will keep running and you may not leave your seat.

7. You are not allowed to bring additional paper into the testing room, so any notes you'd like to take must be written into question sheet. No notes are allowed on the answer sheet.

8. It is not permitted to use tools such as calculators, rulers, formula collections and periodic tables. It is also prohibited to take a mobile phone with you, even if it is switched off.

9. We recommend planning at least five hours for the entire test (i.e. reading the instructions, writing the entire test, and lunch break).

10. It would be advisable to take drinks and snacks with you to have enough energy throughout the test. You should at least have sugary drinks and filling snacks (not just chocolate, but also a sandwich) and water.

THE PRACTICE EXAM

2

CORE TEST: SOLVING QUANTITATIVE PROBLEMS

In this subtest, you'll be presented with a selection of hypothetical everyday scenarios. Your task is to solve these scenarios using the basics of arithmetic (addition, subtraction, multiplication and division). With this test you can estimate how well you can solve simple math problems. Keep in mind that the arithmetic tasks cover just basics, so don't make things more complicated than they are.

The "Solving Quantitative Problems" section consists of **22 questions** that you have to solve in **45 minutes**. Before you start the test on the next page, please take a close look at the following example.

EXAMPLE

The tool factory is open 8 hours a day and produces 4 screwdrivers per hour. How many screwdrivers are produced in 4 days and 5 hours?

(A) 21

(B) 148

(C) 32

(D) 128

Answer: B

On a normal working day, 4 × 8 = 32 screwdrivers are produced.

In 4 days, 4 × 32 = 128 screwdrivers are produced.

In the 5 additional hours: 5 × 4 = 20 screwdrivers are produced.

Add up the numbers and you get the overall result: 128 + 20 = 148 screwdrivers in 4 days and 5 hours.

1.1   Tina goes on vacation and travels 280 *km* from her hometown of Birming-
      ham to Dublin. On the map she uses for her trip, the distance is 35 *cm*. On
      what scale has the map been drawn?

(A) 10 : 800,000

(B) 1 : 800,000

(C) 35 : 280,000

(D) 4 : 400,000

1.2   The insurance company Genico has a total of 120 employees. The compa-
      ny hires 15 assistants and 4 times as many specialist consultants as man-
      aging directors. For how much € in manager salary does Genico plan each
      year if the company pays its managing directors € 20,000 yearly?

(A) € 420,000

(B) € 480,000

(C) € 540,000

(D) € 600,000

1.3   Christina would like to make a trail from her stable, which is 23.42 meters
      north of a river, to her garden house, which is 59.68 meters south of the
      river. How long is the trail?

(A) 44.7 *m*

(B) 83.1 *m*

(C) 92.5 *m*

(D) 59.68 *m*

1.4 Which of the following statements can be inferred from the table?

Distribution of Work Hours in a Factory		
Number of Workers		Number of Hours Worked
32		45 – 50
28		40 – 44
20		35 – 39
26		30 – 34
10		0 – 29
116	TOTAL	4,200

I. The average number of hours worked per worker is less than 40.

II. At least 5 workers worked more than 47 hours.

III. More than half the workers worked at least 40 hours.

    (A) I only

    (B) I and II only

    (C) I and III only

    (D) I, II, and III

1.5   Maureen's taxi drives at 88 *km/h*. The reaction time while driving is 2 seconds. During the journey a cow suddenly appears and the driver brakes. How many meters will Maureen's taxi travel before it fully stops?

(A) 25 *m*

(B) 84.9 *m*

(C) 50 *m*

(D) 48.9 *m*

1.6   Sven takes part in a bicycle race outside of Berlin. It takes him 6 hours and 20 minutes at a constant speed of 48 *km/h* to finish the race. How many kilometers does he cover during this time?

(A) 304 *km*

(B) 320 *km*

(C) 200 *km*

(D) 166.5 *km*

1.7   A boy rides his bicycle with his father. The son drives at 30 *km/h* and his father drives at 15 *km/h*. After 1.5 *km*, the son stops to wait for his father. How many minutes does he have to wait?

(A) 9 *min*

(B) 6 *min*

(C) 3 *min*

(D) 1.5 *min*

1.8 A gas tank has a length of 30 m, a width of 10 m and a height of 20 m. The gas tank is now filled with oxygen at a filling speed of 10 m^3 per minute. How many hours does it take before the tank is full?

(A) 100 h

(B) 17 h

(C) 5 h

(D) 10 h

1.9 The boss of a small construction company knows that his five carpenters need 8 hours to lay tiles on a floor space of 10 m^2. The company receives the order to tile an area of 50 m^2 in a house. To complete the job as quickly as possible, the boss would like to send over all five employees. Unfortunately, one gets sick before they begin. How long does it take the remaining four carpenters to complete the job?

(A) 50 h

(B) 10 h

(C) 30 h

(D) 40 h

1.10 In the diagram below, what is the point on line segment AB that is twice as far from A than it is from B?

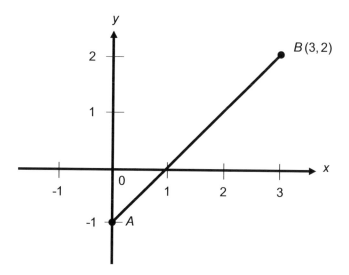

(A) (3; 1)

(B) (2; 1)

(C) (2; -1)

(D) (1.5; 0.5)

1.11 The turnover that the Nussbaum clothing store made in January alone with coats was 2/5 of the December turnover, and the revenue in February was 1/4 of the revenue in January. How big was the revenue in December compared to the average revenue in January and February?

(A) 1/4

(B) 1/2

(C) 4

(D) 2

1.12 Ben rides his bike through Munich. At 9:55 a.m., he sees his friend Georg, who is also traveling by bike. They stop and talk about the upcoming biology exam for 5 minutes. Then Ben rides on at a speed of 14 *km/h* and Georg rides at 9 *km/h* in the opposite direction. After a 120-minute bike, they both reach their destination. Assuming they were moving in a straight line, how many kilometers apart are the two of them at the end of their journey?

(A) 28 *km*

(B) 46 *km*

(C) 18 *km*

(D) 90 *km*

1.13 Six people take a science quiz. Three of the participants will emerge from the quiz as winners. How many different possible combinations of winners are there?

(A) 30

(B) 90

(C) 120

(D) 45

1.14 What is the annual interest payment on debts of € 40,000 if the interest rate is 5.25%?

(A) € 2,100

(B) € 5,000

(C) € 1,200

(D) € 20,000

1.15 Petra wants to visit a friend in Berlin and packs her suitcase. In her closet there are 10 blue, 10 green and 6 red individual socks. She wants to take a pair of socks in each color, but the light has gone out and her closet is completely dark. How many socks does Petra have to get out of the closet so that she has at least one pair of socks in each color?

(A) 6

(B) 10

(C) 20

(D) 22

1.16 The area of the right triangle below is 24 square meters. If $x = y + 2$, what is the value of z, in meters?

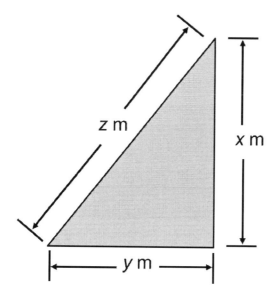

(A) 4 m

(B) 10 m

(C) 2 m

(D) 8 m

1.17 Ms. Schmitt has a recipe for iced tea. 1.2 *g* of sugar must be added per 100 *ml* of tea. She wants to make 175 *ml* of iced tea, how many grams of sugar does she need?

(A) 1.6 *g*

(B) 1.9 *g*

(C) 2.1 *g*

(D) 2.3 *g*

1.18 Rudolf takes out a loan of € 4,000 to buy a scooter. The bank charges 10% interest per year on the loan. How much money in interest will Rudolf have to pay back after one year?

(A) € 400

(B) € 100

(C) € 4,400

(D) € 4,000

1.19 Marina is 11 years older than her younger sister Claudia. Together they are 45 years old. How old is Marina?

(A) 23 years

(B) 25 years

(C) 28 years

(D) 31 years

1.20 Within a month, 60% of the men test takers and 75% of women test takers passed the exact same engineering exam. What percentage of all test participants passed the test if 40% of them were men?

(A) 64%

(B) 69%

(C) 67%

(D) 71%

1.21 The figure below shows a circular flower bed centered at point O, surrounded by a circular path that is 3 meters wide. What is the area of the path, in square meters?

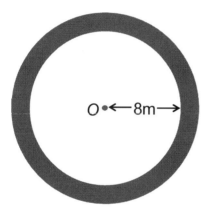

(A) 25 π

(B) 38 π

(C) 55 π

(D) 57 π

2.22 Loretta works on the assembly line of an automobile company. She will be paid x dollars for the first 8 hours of work and y dollars for each hour over-time. She works 11 hours on Monday, 9 hours on Tuesday, 10 hours on Wednesday, 9 hours on Thursday and 8 hours on Friday. What is Loretta's average income for a 5-day week?

(A) $x + 1.4y$

(B) $2x + y$

(C) $(5x + 8y) / 5$

(D) $8x + 1.4y$

Do not turn the page!
Wait for the sign of the test conductor!

STOP

CORE TEST: INFERRING RELATIONSHIPS

Each question in this subtest contains two pairs of words. One of the pairs is missing. Your task is to choose the correct pair of words to fill the gaps. In the missing pair, the relationship between the two words must be analogous (meaning comparable, or identical) to the one between the existing pair. This requires you to identify the nature of the relationship between the two words (the "rule") and select the missing pair based on this.

This subtest is designed to assess your use of logical linguistic thought. You must be able to think about the meanings of the words and then generalize to identify the rule (in other words, to think in an abstract fashion). You must then be able to state the rule in concrete terms in order to find the correct answer.

One example of two pairs of words with analogous relationships would be "tall : short = fat : thin". Both pairs of words are opposites, so the nature of the relationship is the same in each case.

The relative positions of the words on the right- or left-hand side of the colon must be taken into account when solving the analogy.

The test "Inferring Relationships" has **22 questions**, and you'll have **10 minutes** to answer them. The test starts on the next page. Study the example below before you begin.

clock : time = _____ : _____

(A) hour : latitude

(B) thermometer : temperature

(C) weather : climate

(D) tide : moon

Answer: B

Analogy: As a clock measures time, a thermometer measures temperature.

Remember:

All verbs will be given in the form "to + infinitive", e.g. "to run", "to shoot". Many words, like "run", can function as nouns or verbs. If such a word appears without "to", you can assume that the noun form is intended (i.e. "run" in the sense of "I went for a run").

2.1 **stove : kitchen = _____ : _____**

(A) window : bedroom

(B) sink : bathroom

(C) pot : pan

(D) trunk : attic

2.2 **_____ : record label = writer : _____**

(A) sheet of music – chapter

(B) books – songs

(C) musician – publisher

(D) stage – newspaper

2.3 **house : _____ = tree : _____**

(A) village – branch

(B) door – grass

(C) leaf – roof

(D) city – forest

2.4 **_____ : cow = _____ : hen**

(A) milk – eggs

(B) meadow – hay

(C) field – grass

(D) mare – cock

2.5 _____ : _____ = calm : quiet

    (A) dramatic : believable

    (B) daring : courageous

    (C) mysterious : hidden

    (D) weak : pathetic

2.6 _____ : everything = few : _____

    (A) more – quantity

    (B) nothing – a lot

    (C) mostly – oftentimes

    (D) much – all

2.7 trout : _____ = _____ : car

    (A) salmon – sports car

    (B) sea – streets

    (C) animal – truck

    (D) fish – Ferrari

2.8 _____ : _____ = chess : board game

    (A) emerald : gemstone

    (B) carrot : salad

    (C) tree : maple

    (D) rose twig : rose

2.9 fruit : _____ = animal : _____

    (A) cucumber – tree

    (B) peach – hamster

    (C) car – motorcycle

    (D) school – students

2.10 _____ : _____ = lake : body of water

    (A) fruit : banana

    (B) humid : waterway

    (C) tropical : climate

    (D) hot : sun

2.11 ocean : _____ = _____ : birds

    (A) thunder – wind

    (B) fish – sky

    (C) waves – cloud

    (D) water – moon

2.12 cork : bottle = _____ : _____

    (A) door : entrance

    (B) wine : beer

    (C) house : basement

    (D) glass : cork

2.13 _____ : night = _____ : leaf

(A) Moon - beautiful

(B) black – hope

(C) dark – green

(D) quiet – swoosh

2.14 _____ : _____ = bird : sky

(A) human : earth

(B) to sing : voice

(C) feather : wing

(D) parrot : angel

2.15 train : _____ = _____ : cooling

(A) cookie – tasty

(B) cosmos – silence

(C) transport – ice

(D) hit – strength

2.16 _____ : verdict = scientist : _____

(A) lawyer – insight

(B) judge – discovery

(C) analyst - diagnose

(D) exam – assignment

2.17 _____ : grabbed = _____ : let

   (A) to record – to read

   (B) to grab – to let

   (C) to let – to walk

   (D) to grasp – to love

2.18 stood : _____ = _____ **: to be**

   (A) was standing – am

   (B) stands – was

   (C) to stand – was

   (D) stands – would

2.19 to shout : _____ **= to ask :** _____

   (A) to bellow – to speak

   (B) to talk – to challenge

   (C) to discuss – to whisper

   (D) heard – answered

2.20 _____ **: to talk = cold :** _____

   (A) silence – warm-up

   (B) room – shivering

   (C) mouth – winter

   (D) quietness – cool

2.21 warm : hot = _____ : _____

(A) interested : clever

(B) stupid : smart

(C) wise : intelligent

(D) clever : brilliant

2.22 _____ : uncomfortable = devotional : _____

(A) disagreeable – friendly

(B) delicious – scurrilous

(C) unendurable – caring

(D) friendly – mean-spirited

Do not turn the page!
Wait for the sign of the test conductor!

STOP

CORE TEST: COMPLETING PATTERNS

Please take the time to read the following instructions, for which you are given 5 additional minutes. **At the end of these 5 minutes, the test representative will give you the sign to start solving the questions in this section.**

In this section of the test you will be dealing with lines, circles, squares and other geometric bodies, which are arranged in a certain pattern and in a square matrix. You have to recognize and complete the pattern by selecting the correct picture (options A to F) for the last free box.

The patterns (or "rules") only apply from left to right or from top to bottom – never diagonally. However, you sometimes have to identify up to three different rules to solve the matrix. And it can also happen that a pattern applies from top to bottom and simultaneously from left to right.

The "Completing Patterns" test consists of **22 questions** for which you have **20 minutes**.

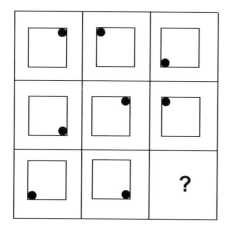

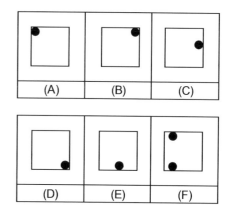

Answer: B

How should the pattern be read? From left to right →

Shape: The dot changes position.

Direction / Orientation: The dot moves counterclockwise within the four corners.

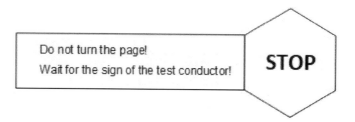

Do not turn the page!
Wait for the sign of the test conductor!

STOP

3.1

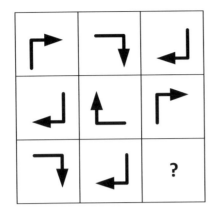 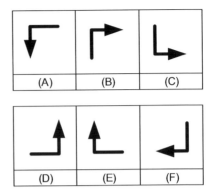

3.2

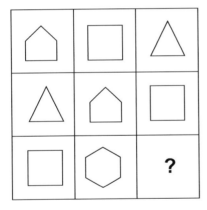 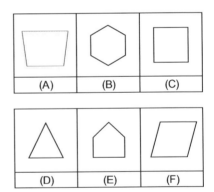

3.3

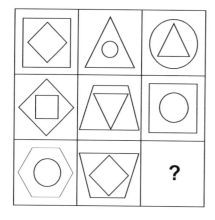

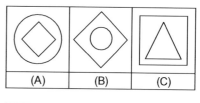

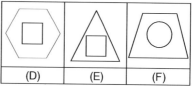

3.4

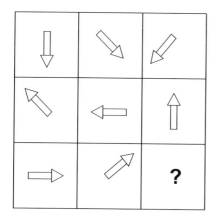

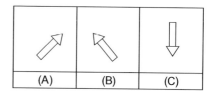

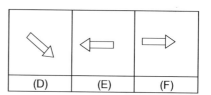

3.5

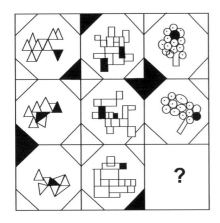
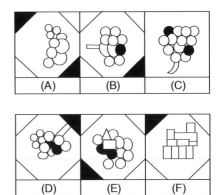

3.6

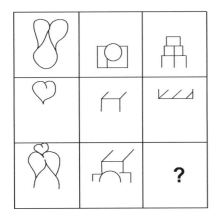
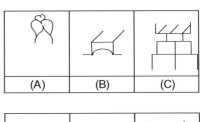
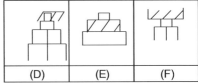

3.7

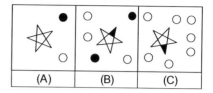

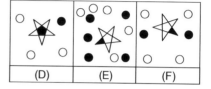

3.8

3.9

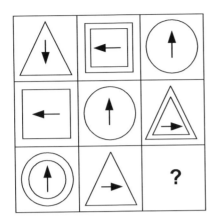

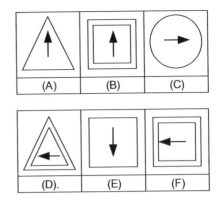

3.10

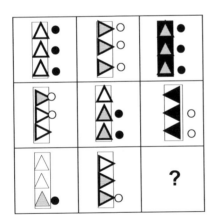

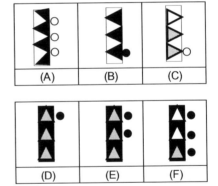

3.11

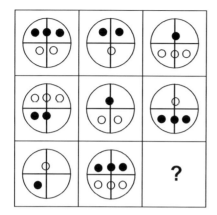

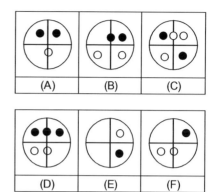

3.12

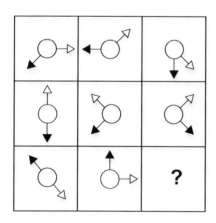

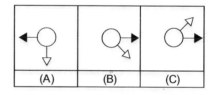

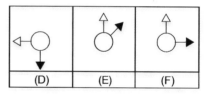

3.13

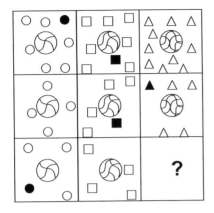 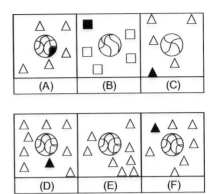

3.14

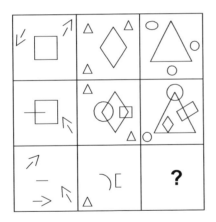 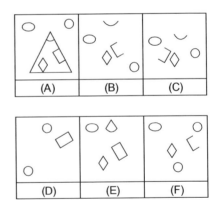

Practice test – Core Test and Humanities-, Cultural Studies and Social Sciences

3.15

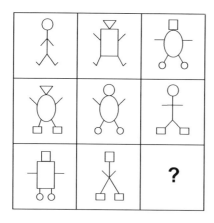

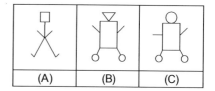

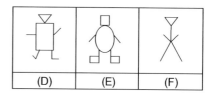

3.16

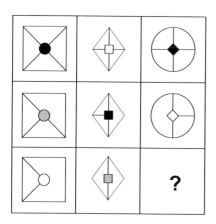

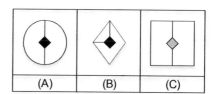

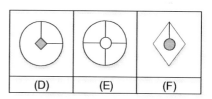

3.17

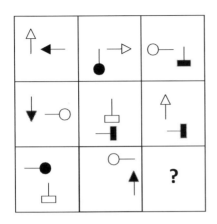

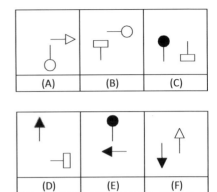

3.18

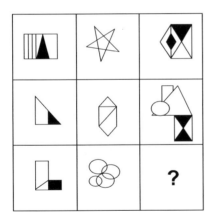

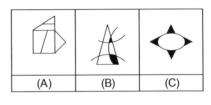

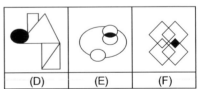

3.19

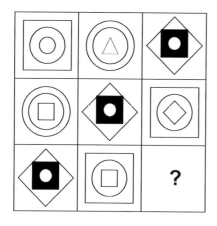

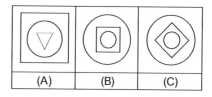

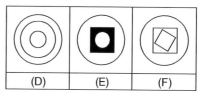

3.20

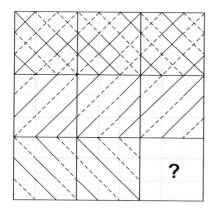

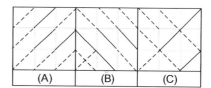

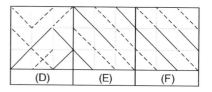

3.21

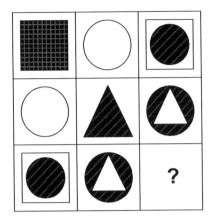

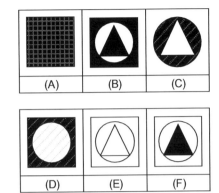

3.22

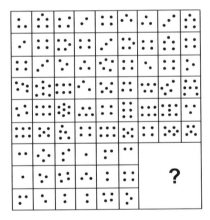

Do not turn the page!
Wait for the sign of the test conductor!

STOP

CORE TEST: CONTINUING NUMERICAL SERIES

Please take the time to read the following instructions, for which you are given 5 additional minutes. **At the end of these 5 minutes, the test representative will give you the sign to start solving the questions in this section**.

In this subtest, you'll see a sequence of numbers that follows a specific rule or pattern. Your task is to determine the rule and apply it in order to fill in the missing number. This subtest is designed to test logical thought in relation to numbers. No special mathematical knowledge is required to answer the questions – you simply need to be able to add, subtract, multiply and divide.

The test "Continuing Numerical Series" has **22 questions** and you'll have **25 minutes** to answer them.

EXAMPLE

| 31 | 32 | 34 | 35 | 37 | 38 | ? |

Answer: 40

Explanation: The first two terms are 31 and 32; therefore, the difference between the first and second terms is +1. The difference between the second and the third terms is +2. For the fourth and fifth terms, the difference reverts back to +1. As we proceed along the sequence, it becomes evident that it follows the pattern given below.

The rule for this numerical series:

| + 1 | + 2 | + 1 | + 2 | + 1 | + 2 |

On the answer sheet, mark the digits that appear in the solution number. If the number is negative, please mark the "–" on the answer sheet as well as the digits. The order of the digits does NOT matter.

On the answer sheet, 40 would be entered in the following way:

	–	0	1	2	3	4	5	6	7	8	9
	☐	☒	☐	☐	☐	☒	☐	☐	☐	☐	☐

| −200 | −50 | −46 | −184 | −188 | −47 | ? |

Answer: −43

Explanation: We can establish a relationship between the first two numbers by dividing -200 by 4 to get -50. The third number in the sequence is 46, so this time 4 is added to -50. The fourth number in the sequence is -184, which we get by multiplying the third number by 4. If you subtract 4 from -184, you get the -188, the fifth number. This means, the pattern here consists in performing various arithmetic operations with the number 4, as shown below.

The rule for this numerical series:

| / 4 | + 4 | × 4 | − 4 | / 4 | + 4 |

On the answer sheet, -43 would be entered in the following way:

	−	0	1	2	3	4	5	6	7	8	9
	☒	☐	☐	☐	☒	☒	☐	☐	☐	☐	☐

Do not turn the page!
Wait for the sign of the test conductor!

STOP

4.1	126	252	255	510	513	1026	?
4.2	–9	–6	–7	–4	–5	–2	?
4.3	–23	–21	–42	–40	–80	–78	?
4.4	10	11	22	25	100	105	?
4.5	34	39	41	46	55	60	?
4.6	56	63	72	83	96	111	?
4.7	–112	–96	–121	–105	–129	–113	?
4.8	234	236	221	225	213	219	?

| **4.9** | 20 | 11 | 44 | 36 | 144 | 137 | ? |

| **4.10** | 50 | 45 | 30 | 25 | 10 | 5 | ? |

| **4.11** | 78 | 76 | 38 | 36 | 18 | 16 | ? |

| **4.12** | −81 | −82 | −79 | −80 | −76 | −77 | ? |

| **4.13** | −280 | −140 | −135 | −45 | −40 | −10 | ? |

| **4.14** | 660 | 670 | 680 | 650 | 660 | 670 | ? |

| **4.15** | 25 | 32 | 30 | 30 | 36 | 33 | ? |

| **4.16** | 6 | 6 | 12 | 36 | 144 | 720 | ? |

| **4.17** | 12 | 8 | 56 | 8 | 4 | 28 | ? |

| **4.18** | 11 | 8 | 24 | 27 | 9 | 6 | ? |

| **4.19** | −27 | −30 | −15 | −45 | −48 | −24 | ? |

| **4.20** | 108 | 112 | 28 | 32 | 8 | 12 | ? |

| **4.21** | −15 | −12 | −9 | −6 | −3 | 0 | ? |

| **4.22** | 80 | 40 | 36 | 108 | 54 | 50 | ? |

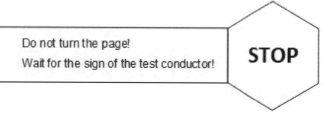

Do not turn the page!
Wait for the sign of the test conductor!

STOP

TEST MODULE: UNDERSTANDING AND INTERPRETING TEXTS

In the section "Understanding and Interpreting Texts" you have to understand the content of texts, interpret them correctly and then answer two questions with two parts each about what you have read.

You will receive a series of short texts of approximately 100-200 words each which you have to read. In our exercises, the texts are often a little longer. They are followed by two tasks, each of which checks whether you understood the content of the text and can draw the correct conclusions from it.

The "Understanding and Interpreting Texts" section consists of **22 questions** that you have to solve in **45 minutes**. Before you start the exam on the next page, please take a close look at the following example.

EXAMPLE

Dr. Manfred Bischoff is chairman of the supervisory board of the German automobile company Daimler AG. The following is a brief summary of his lecture on "Globalization: What are the challenges for maintaining German competitiveness?"

Dr. Bischoff first addressed the question of where Germany currently stands economically and to what extent we live in a globalized world. The answer to the first of these questions, according to Dr. Bischoff, is that Germany has so far improved economically. In answering the second question, he gave four reasons to support his claim that globalization, or the increasing interdependence of individual countries, is now an all-powerful force. First, free trade and the free market are now rep-resented worldwide. The second reason is the global flow of free capital. The third reason is that global logistics costs have reached a gratifying low, which is evidence of the efficiency of the economy. Finally, the fourth reason is that a global workforce has now formed against the background of the globalization of the labor market.

Nevertheless, Dr. Bischoff pointed out that there is criticism of the indebted German government and the rest of the world. According to him, large companies in the future will rely on a highly qualified workforce, investments in education and research, better connections between universities and industry, a universal change in values, an ethical awareness, and the cooperation of the functional elites.

Which of the two following statements is or are correct according to the above text?

I. The decrease in logistics costs was a factor that supported the ubiquity of globalization.

II. The globalization of the education market has led to the creation of a global workforce.

    (A) Only statement I is correct.

    (B) Only statement II is correct.

    (C) Both statements are correct.

    (D) Neither of the two statements are correct.

Answer: A

Statement I is correct, because one of the reasons given in the text as to why "globalization (...) is now an all-powerful force", is "that global logistics costs have reached a gratifying low."

Statement II is wrong, because it was the globalization of the labor market, not that of the education market, that led to the formation of a global workforce.

TEXT FOR 5.1. AND 5.2.

The Olympic Games originated in Olympia, Greece, and most textbooks list 776 BC as the year of the first official games. This assertion is based on inscriptions in Olympia that list the winners of a footrace held in 776 BC and every four years afterwards; however, many scholars believe that the games had actually been happening in some form for many years before that. According to tradition, the first champion of the games was a cook named Coroebus, who took the title by winning the sole event at the time – a 192-metre (210-yard) run. Held at the sanctuary of Zeus in Olympia, the games continued to grow for the next 1200 years and eventually came to feature running, pentathlon, boxing, wrestling, pankration, and equestrian events. In addition to being a sporting event, the Ancient Olympics also featured many ceremonies and ritual sacrifices to honor the god Zeus. In AD 393, a Roman emperor named Theodosius I, who was Christian, abolished the games due to their connection with pagan beliefs. The Olympic tradition was revived in the 1800s, and the first modern games were held in 1896.

5.1. **Which of the two following statements is or are correct according to the above text?**

I. Most experts believe that the idea for the Olympic games was thought up in 776 BC.

II. It was more than a thousand years before the games were brought back to life.

(A) Only statement I is correct.

(B) Only statement II is correct.

(C) Both statements are correct.

(D) Neither of the two statements are correct.

5.2. **Which of the two following statements is or are correct according to the above text?**

I. The Ancient Olympics was both a sporting and a religious event.

II. Like the modern Olympics, the ancient Olympics featured athletes from all over the world.

(A) Only statement I is correct.

(B) Only statement II is correct.

(C) Both statements are correct.

(D) Neither of the two statements are correct.

TEXT FOR 5.3. AND 5.4.

The rationale behind liberal thinking is illustrated in the following (originally German) quote: "Liberalism leaves people in peace, without abandoning them completely." The four Freiburg Theses were adopted on October 27th, 1971 at the Federal Party Convention of the FDP (Free Democratic Party, a classical liberal party in Germany) after the FDP received only 5.8% of the vote at the 1969 Bundestag elections (German parliamentary elections).

The first thesis states that people should be given precedence over institutions and that the preservation and development of the individual and the concept of plurality should be promoted within human societies. The second thesis says that liberalism stands for progress and reason. According to the third thesis, we are all part of society, but "society must not be permitted to be everything." The fourth thesis supports a reform of the capitalistic system to abolish trends promoting the accumulation of wealth in only a few hands. At its core, a liberal society should serve people, promote an increase in production and ensure the protection of the needy and the environment.

5.3. **Which of the two following statements is or are correct according to the above text?**

I.   Environmental protection is considered to be of subordinate importance within a liberal society.

II. One of the functions of a liberal society is to protect the needy.

(A) Only statement I is correct.

(B) Only statement II is correct.

(C) Both statements are correct.

(D) Neither of the two statements are correct.

5.4. **Which of the two following statements is or are correct according to the above text?**

I.   According to the third thesis, the German federal chancellor Angela Merkel is a part of the society.

II. The result of the 1969 Bundestag election was the worst in the FDP's history.

(A) Only statement I is correct.

(B) Only statement II is correct.

(C) Both statements are correct.

(D) Neither of the two statements are correct.

TEXT FOR 5.5. AND 5.6.

The impact of human activity on the planet is putting an increasing number of animal species at risk of extinction. Though extinction is a natural process that has occurred throughout the earth's history, studies show that man-made factors such as climate change, hunting and poaching, fishing practices, pollution, and loss of habitat are accelerating the process and creating unprecedented numbers of endangered species. Some of the most at-risk species include tigers, polar bears, penguins and various kinds of fish. Many insects are also threatened – a recent assessment of European wild bee species found that 9.2% were in danger of becoming extinct. Of all the ways that humans are changing the planet, the temperature increase due to global warming is thought to be the most dangerous. If the planet warms by an average of 3 degrees Celsius, scientists predict that 8.5% of the world's species will be in danger of ceasing to exist.

5.5. **Which of the two following statements is or are correct according to the above text?**

I. Just over 9% of all wild bee species worldwide are thought to be at risk of extinction.

II. Bad fishing practices are responsible for the fact that many kinds of fish are now endangered.

(A) Only statement I is correct.

(B) Only statement II is correct.

(C) Both statements are correct.

(D) Neither of the two statements are correct.

5.6. **Which of the two following statements is or are correct according to the above text?**

I. The temperature increase due to global warming is generally considered to be a more significant threat to animals than hunting and poaching.

II. If the earth's temperature rises by an average of 3 degrees Celsius, the number of animal species will be reduced by 8.5%.

(A) Only statement I is correct.

(B) Only statement II is correct.

(C) Both statements are correct.

(D) Neither of the two statements are correct.

TEXT FOR 5.7. AND 5.8.

Once upon a time, a lion was sleeping deeply and peacefully in the jungle. As he slept, a small mouse passed by. Without realizing what he was doing, the mouse ran over the lion, tickled him and woke him up. Immediately, the lion trapped the mouse under his big paw and opened his mouth to swallow him whole. "Pardon me, Mr. Lion!" squeaked the mouse. "Please forgive me. I'll make sure to never do such a thing again, and I'll never forget your kindness. Perhaps one day I'll be able to repay you." The lion smiled to himself. He didn't see how such a small creature could ever be of any use to a lion, but he was so amused by the mouse's request that he let him go. It just so happened that some hours later, some hunters passed by, captured the lion and tied him to a tree while they looked for a wagon to carry him home. The mouse passed by once again, saw the sad plight of the lion, and set about chewing through the ropes. Soon, the lion was free and the mouse was beaming with pride. "Did I not tell you I'd pay you back someday?" he asked the lion. "Yes," agreed the lion, smiling widely, "you were right!"

5.7. **Which of the two following statements is or are correct according to the above text?**

I. The mouse didn't mean to annoy the lion.

II. The lion let the mouse go because he was expecting to be repaid.

    (A) Only statement I is correct.

    (B) Only statement II is correct.

    (C) Both statements are correct.

    (D) Neither of the two statements are correct.

5.8. **Which of the two following statements is or are correct according to the above text?**

I. The lion would definitely have died if the mouse hadn't saved him.

II. The lion will never think of eating the mouse again.

    (A) Only statement I is correct.

    (B) Only statement II is correct.

    (C) Both statements are correct.

    (D) Neither of the two statements are correct.

TEXT FOR 5.9. AND 5.10.

The article "Student Writing Guidance is Professional and Personalized" (originally written in German) discusses a research project from the Writing Centre at the European University Viadrina in Frankfurt (Oder), Germany. Within the student-writing-guidance project, students seeking guidance were offered the help of other students. The goal of the project was to bring about an increase in students' writing competence. Various concepts were deployed in an attempt to achieve this, including "help through self-help", the exchange of experiences, emotions and knowledge, and active engagement with individual writing projects. The project's success was evaluated in a study which compiled the results of qualitative content analyses and problem-focused interviews. The goal of qualitative content analysis is the systematic processing of communication content that must adhere to a certain form. It does not evaluate the content but is instead aimed at creating a representation of formal aspects and latent meaning. A category system was developed on the results of the qualitative content analysis and used to measure how the student writing guidance was received by the guidance-seeking students. The guidance-seekers were asked how they entered and exited the guidance session, how they perceived the session, what they noticed about it, how they felt during and after the session and whether the session triggered anything new in relation to them as individuals or their writing.

5.9. Which of the two following statements is or are correct according to the above text?

I.   The project's success was predominantly evaluated with problem-focused interviews.

II. Qualitative content analysis arose out of the category system.

(A) Only statement I is correct.

(B) Only statement II is correct.

(C) Both statements are correct.

(D) Neither of the two statements are correct.

5.10. Which of the two following statements is or are correct according to the above text?

I.   The purpose of qualitative content analysis is the graphical processing of communication content.

II. Qualitative content analysis goes beyond merely compiling information about the actual content.

(A) Only statement I is correct.

(B) Only statement II is correct.

(C) Both statements are correct.

(D) Neither of the two statements are correct.

TEXT FOR 5.11. AND 5.12.

At the beginning of an assignment, David always reads the instructions carefully and then skims through the text to get an overview before starting the first question. When he comes across a problem he cannot solve, he simply skips over the problem and goes to the next question. When he finishes the work, he looks at the skipped problem once more and, if necessary, he asks the teacher for help. When learning new things, he relies primarily on memory and observation – I can tell that he is more able to memorize information when he can see it. When it comes to German class, David quietly follows the lesson – quite in contrast to his behavior during natural history class. Though he also follows the lesson, in natural history he talks much more with his fellow students and shares jokes, most of which he comes up with on his own. The subject of the "central nervous system" is one that particularly appeals to him. David finds it easy to draw logical conclusions, which helps him excel in fact-based subjects like math and science. However, he finds it difficult to utilize his creativity.

5.11. **Which of the two following statements is or are correct according to the above text?**

    I.   David finds it easy to make use of his musical talent.

    II.   David prefers to see and hear things in order to remember them.

        (A) Only statement I is correct.

        (B) Only statement II is correct.

        (C) Both statements are correct.

        (D) Neither of the two statements are correct.

5.12. **Which of the two following statements is or are correct according to the above text?**

    I.   David is always quiet during German classes.

    II.   David knows exactly what the central nervous system is

        (A) Only statement I is correct.

        (B) Only statement II is correct.

        (C) Both statements are correct.

        (D) Neither of the two statements are correct.

TEXT FOR 5.13. AND 5.14.

"Bangkok," a photography series which was produced in 2011 by Andreas Gurksy, is radiant. What the nine portrait formats of „Bangkok," about three by two meters each, actually have to do with Bangkok is not optically conclusive; Bangkok cannot be seen in "Bangkok." There is no palace and no Buddha, just water and water endlessly, with streaks or mosaics of light, which the dark, unsettling ground throws back, sometimes as jagged, glistening verticals, over which grey shades and orange colored reflections run parallel, sometimes as amorphous spots appearing to fly. The ground is black and white and in between there are swarming, small, colorful, dark yellow, turquoise and pink spots and sprinklings.

Nothing can be seen of the city, just the river Chao Phraya which gracefully but cumbersomely winds its way through and, as suggested by the title "Bangkok", has completely absorbed it. Just like other rivers in other megacities, the Chao Phraya carries filth: pollution – the waste of civilizations. The water is black, and does it really flow? It could be lava or tar, oil or mud.

Source: http://www.faz.net/aktuell/feuilleton/kunst/andreas-gursky-alles-im-fluss-11938416.html; Accessed 24.07.2019

5.13. Which of the two following statements is or are correct according to the above text?

I.   The photography series "Bangkok" from 2011 is three by four meters large.

II. In the photography series, a darker side of Bangkok can be seen: Only the river is depicted in which a large amount of rubbish can be seen.

(A) Only statement I is correct.

(B) Only statement II is correct.

(C) Both statements are correct.

(D) Neither of the two statements are correct.

5.14. Which of the two following statements is or are correct according to the above text?

I.   You can see streaks, mosaics and numerous amorphous forms in the pictures.

II. You can see the city of Bangkok in "Bangkok".

(A) Only statement I is correct.

(B) Only statement II is correct.

(C) Both statements are correct.

(D) Neither of the two statements are correct.

TEXT FOR 5.15. AND 5.16.

Time and again, we hear of the illegal and immoral acts committed by individuals within and between companies. This raises questions regarding the motives for such acts. We must question whether the market economy promotes moral values, whether it creates incentives for immoral behavior, whether it drives immoral behavior in favor of profit maximization and to the detriment of ethics, whether it is possible for companies to curb this behavior using internally prescribed moral codes and whether companies actually have an interest in adhering to their own moral codes or will always favor of profit when faced with a moral dilemma.

5.15. **Which of the two following statements is or are correct according to the above text?**

    I.   Banks are denounced as being especially immoral.

    II. The market economy promotes moral values.

        (A) Only statement I is correct.

        (B) Only statement II is correct.

        (C) Both statements are correct.

        (D) Neither of the two statements are correct.

5.16. **Which of the two following statements is or are correct according to the above text?**

    I.   There are no obviously fully-effective solutions to solving the issue mentioned in the text.

    II. The problem relates only to dealings between companies.

        (A) Only statement I is correct.

        (B) Only statement II is correct.

        (C) Both statements are correct.

        (D) Neither of the two statements are correct.

TEXT FOR 5.17. AND 5.18.

Dillig: What is special about the scene of German sports clubs?

Schulke: With 90,000 sports clubs today in Germany, there are simply a lot of them. This is not the case in other countries that also have a lively club scene such as Sweden, Switzerland or the USA. Most clubs emerged from the 19th century gymnastics movement. It all started with the fact that Friedrich Ludwig Jahn, later to become the "father of gymnastics", set up a place for physical exercises in Hasenheide in 1811.

Dillig: A kind of outdoor gym.

Schulke: Exactly. The sporting equipment are comparable. This was an open and public space, anyone could come here, no matter what age, what class. Everyone could individually choose what exercises to do. The motto of the French revolution "Liberty, Equality, Fraternity" was lived here and led to the then completely new construct of a "club." There had never been anything like this in human history.

Dillig: Today, many people see Jahn as a nationalist and militarist.

Schulke: Yes, also because the Nazis claimed him for themselves. But that is unfair. Jahn was a democrat, an educated pedagogue and, to the extent that he was a soldier, he was a representative of military training, but only in accordance with a war of protection, not a war of attack. He believed that Germany, which had been attacked by Napoleon and oppressed by its standing army, should be able to defend itself. But what he established with his gym fields was the opposite of the "cadaver obedience" that still prevailed in Frederick the Great's day. (...)

Source: First part of the interviews »In Sportvereinen war die Willkommenskultur schon immer selbstver-ständlich«, 26.07.2016, http://sz-magazin.sueddeutsche.de/texte/anzeigen/44831, Accessed 27.07.2019

5.17. **Which of the two following statements is or are correct according to the above text?**

I.   The first gym was built in Hasenheide for physical exercises at the beginning of the 19th century and was a kind of open-air gym.

II.   The sports gym in which everyone could choose individual exercises arose from the German model of democracy.

    (A) Only statement I is correct.

    (B) Only statement II is correct.

    (C) Both statements are correct.

    (D) Neither of the two statements are correct.

5.18. **Which of the two following statements is or are correct according to the above text?**

I.   The term "club" was a new invention and stems from the French revolution.

II.   Jahn was a nationalist representative of military training.

    (A) Only statement I is correct.

    (B) Only statement II is correct.

    (C) Both statements are correct.

    (D) Neither of the two statements are correct.

TEXT FOR 5.19. AND 5.20.

The Luise Meyer High School in Germany offers four different pathways through its sub-departments: the classical high school, the music-oriented high school, the high school for art and the high school for languages. The school was renovated a few years ago and the new facilities and spacious premises contribute to its impressive effect. The school is decorated in an interesting and creative way with pictures from the art lyceum. The school attaches great importance to participating in a variety of non-school activities. As the demand for enrollment in the Luise Meyer School is usually very high, some applicants are forced to go to other schools. This is the case despite the size of the school premises of the Luise Meyer High School.

5.19. Which of the two following statements is or are correct according to the above text?

I. The renovation has helped the school to make a good impression.

II. More and more children are attending high schools, so that the demand for places at the Luise Meyer High School is constantly increasing.

(A) Only statement I is correct.

(B) Only statement II is correct.

(C) Both statements are correct.

(D) Neither of the two statements are correct.

5.20. Which of the two following statements is or are correct according to the above text?

I. The facilities and the spacious premises are both a result of the renovation.

II. The Luise Meyer High School has a very creative teaching program.

(A) Only statement I is correct.

(B) Only statement II is correct.

(C) Both statements are correct.

(D) Neither of the two statements are correct.

TEXT FOR 5.21. AND 5.22.

The decline of the print media has been a much-debated topic in recent years. With increasing competition from digital media, newspapers are faced with rising production costs, a decrease in advertising sales and an unprecedented decline in circulation. Of these factors, the decrease in advertising revenue is by far the biggest problem that newspapers have faced. In 2014, researchers in the United States found that print advertising revenue was the lowest since the "Newspaper Association of America" began collecting industry data in 1950. Around 350 newspapers in the United States have stopped operating. A number of newspaper professionals still believe that printed publications will play an important role in the future of news organizations. However, experts like Aron Pilhofer, the leading digital editor of the British newspaper "The Guardian", believe that a further decline will be "a matter of fact".

5.21. Which of the two following statements is or are correct according to the above text?

I.   The expense for newspaper printing contributed to the decline.

II. Most people in the newspaper industry think that print media will continue to play an important role in the future.

(A) Only statement I is correct.

(B) Only statement II is correct.

(C) Both statements are correct.

(D) Neither of the two statements is correct.

5.22. Which of the two following statements is or are correct according to the above text?

I.   Over 300 newspapers have gone bankrupt in the United States since the decline of the industry began.

II. In 2014, print ad sales were lower than ever before.

(A) Only statement I is correct.

(B) Only statement II is correct.

(C) Both statements are correct.

(D) Neither of the two statements is correct.

Do not turn the page!
Wait for the sign of the test conductor!

STOP

TEST MODULE: USING REPRESENTATIONS SYSTEMS FLEXI-BLY

This subtest evaluates how well test takers can transfer information read in texts to an illustration or symbolic representation. The questions of this subtest will pull the most important terms or variables out of the text and relate them to one another. Processes are connected with arrows, and if there are causal effects, these arrows are deemed positive (+) or negative (-). For example, if one variable (X) has a positive effect on another (Y), that means that would be "the higher X, than the higher Y" and "the lower X, than the lower Y." Similarly, a negative effect means that "the higher X, than the lower Y" or "the lower X, than the higher Y". Other arrows or lines may also appear, which are then explained in the question.

Typically, the questions are presented in one of the following ways:

- A text is given and a corresponding visual depiction is presented. Correction of the depiction is required.

- A text is given and test takers must select the correct depiction out of four possible answers.

- A text is given and a corresponding partial visual depiction is presented. Test takers must supplement the depiction.

For this section of the test, no prior information is required. In fact, only information that is presented within the text should be used when answering the questions.

This subtest has **22 questions** for which are allotted **55 minutes**.

Anuran is a class of amphibian that contains approximately 5,400 species of frogs and toads. Typically, anurans are divided into three suborders: Archaeobatrachia, Mesobatrachia and Neobatrachia. The most primitive types of frogs belong to the Archaeobatrachia suborder. This suborder contains only 28 species that share certain characteristics unique to Anuran. They are largely found in South-East Asia and New Zealand and include frogs belonging to the Bombinatoridae, Discoglossidae and Leiopelmatidae families. Mesobatrachia was only categorized as a suborder in 1993, and varieties from its 168 species can be found all around the world. The frogs and toads belonging to this suborder include members of the Pipidae and Megophryidae family groups. The Pipidae family is comprised of 30 species and is characterized by a lack of tongue and vocal cords. The Neobatrachia suborder contains the most advanced and apomorphic frogs and toads of the three suborders. This group includes over 5000 species, equating to 96% of all living Anurans, which are divided into numerous family groups including the Bufonidae, Brachycephalidae and Dendrobatidae.

Which of the following diagrams shows the correct allocation of superordinate terms and subordinate terms?

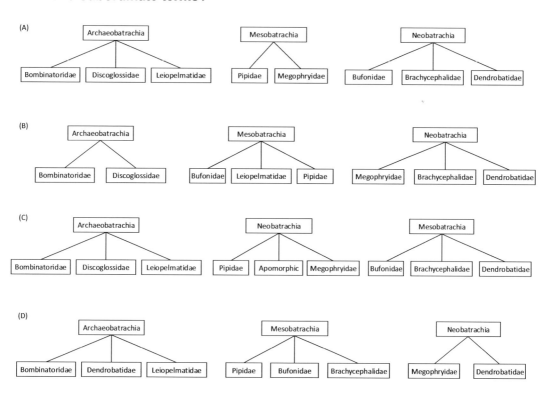

Answer: A

The text mentions three suborders of Anurans, namely Archaeobatrachia, Mesobatrachia and Neobatrachia. Then the respective family groups are described:

Bombinatoridae, Discoglossidae and Leiopelmatidae belong to the suborder Archaeobatrachia.

Pipidae and Megophryidae belong to the suborder Mesobatrachia.

Bufonidae, Brachycephalidae, and Dendrobatidae belong to the suborder Neobatrachia.

Answer A is therefore correct.

6.1

The history of coffee starts in Ethiopia: Coffee was most likely a recognized drink there by the 9th century. It was not until the 14th century that coffee reached Arabia, then spreading to Persia and the Ottoman Empire. The first European to report experiencing coffee was a physician from Augsburg who encountered the drink while visiting Aleppo in 1582. Other travelers began to bring coffee back to Europe as a souvenir, and in the 17th century, coffee houses opened in Venice and then in London, Vienna and finally Paris and Bremen.

Which of the following statements is or are correct?

I. The following order applies to the worldwide distribution of coffee:

II. The following order applies to the European-wide distribution of coffee:

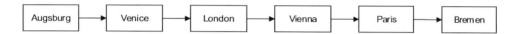

(A) Only statement (I) is correct.

(B) Only statement (II) is correct.

(C) Both statements are correct.

(D) Neither of the two statements is correct.

For 6.2 and 6.3

Elizabeth is about to enter Middle School, and her school offers several different sports teams which she might join. But she has to choose which. She can join one team per season, and there are the fall, winter, and spring seasons. She knows that in the winter she wants to join the swim team, because she hates basketball and doesn't think she'd like cheerleading (and wrestling is only offered to boys). For the other seasons, it isn't so easy to narrow it down to just one sport. Elizabeth would like to do cross county because her new boyfriend Tommy does cross county and they could hang out, plus cross county training would prepare her well for track, an all-girls team in the spring which her friends Ashley and Maria are on. But Elizabeth really likes volleyball, and it interferes with cross county. Then there is also the choice between track and lacrosse. Elizabeth thinks lacrosse is a more fun sport, but most of the people who play lacrosse also play field hockey, and she wouldn't want to feel left out during field hockey season which is at the same time as volleyball.

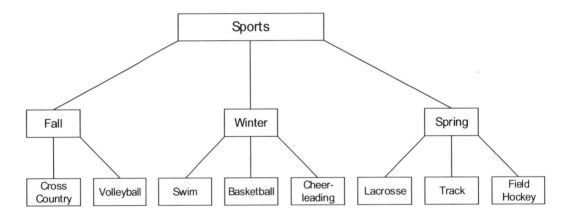

6.2 Which of the following two statements about this diagram is or are correct?

I. At least one of the sports mentioned within the text is not found within the graph.

II. One of the spring sports should be a fall sport.

    (A) Only statement (I) is correct.

    (B) Only statement (II) is correct.

    (C) Both statements are correct.

(D) Neither of the two statements is correct.

6.3 Which three sports might Tommy compete in?

(A) Cross country, swim, track

(B) Cross country, wrestling, track

(C) Volleyball, swim, lacrosse

(D) Cross country, basketball, lacrosse

6.4

Tea is a hot, infusion-based drink, traditionally defined by its degree of oxidation. Green tea has no intended oxidation, whereas black tea has undergone complete oxidation. Typically, European teas are named after the area in which the leaves were grown, and tea-makers can get quite creative with this. Take, for example, the German tea company Teehaus Hermann. They have teas called Morning-Dew-Sunfield and Rose-Whisper, both of which are green teas with floral notes. They also sell a black tea, the East Frisian tea, which basically an Indian tea. A British tea company, Sussex Hillside, has similarly creative names. For example, the Golden Yunnan: grown on Mango Flower Island, this black tea's unique floral fragrances set it apart from teas grown on the mainland. Sussex Hillside also produces the Gunpowder tea, which is also organic and grown in china, but unlike the Golden Yunnan, it is green. Another popular tea company called Fair Tea only produces fair-trade tea. It sells the Keegun Coungo, characterized by its sweet, mild taste and even black texture. Its tea Warashino Bio, on the other hand, is fruity and fresh and, like other black teas, contains a lot of vitamin C. Fair Tea also sells the black tea Terry Lupsung Souching, which offers a unique, nuanced taste, as only resin-rich woods are used in its roasting.

Which of the following diagrams shows the correct allocation of superordinate terms and subordinate terms?

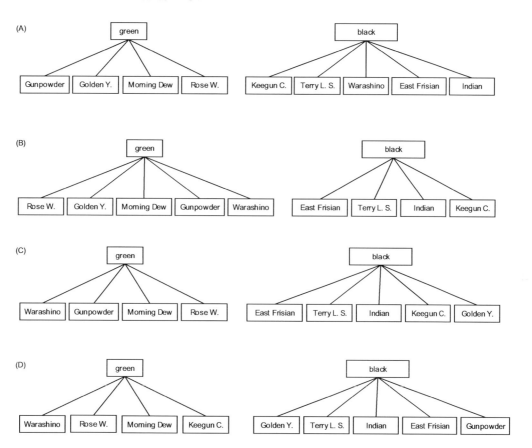

For 6.5 and 6.6

Martin dreams of having a Tesla. Although he loves his current car, a Lexus, he has become increasingly aware of his carbon footprint and he would feel better driving an all-electric car. He did once drive a Prius, but only for a few months before getting his Volkswagen Bug, which he took with him to college. When Martin was younger (before his environmental concerns) he dreamed of having a Porsche, but he also thought any car would be better than his 1992 Buick Roadmaster. The car he learned to drive in (and again had to drive in college as well, after his Volkswagen Bug broke down), the Buick Roadmaster was a sturdy car, but he could never get it to stop smelling like pizza and cigarettes. As a college graduation present, Martin's parents gave him a Honda Civic, and although it was no Porsche, he greatly appreciated it and it lasted him many years.

6.5 Which diagram shows the correct timeline of Martin's cars?

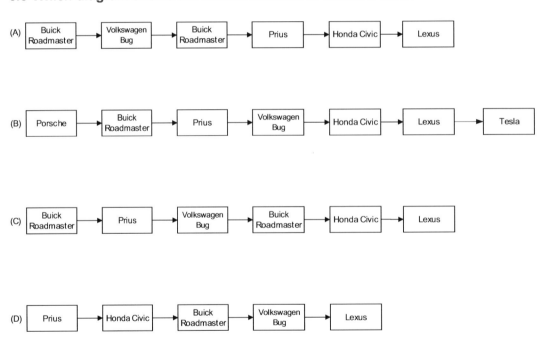

6.6 Suppose Martin has also driven two loaner cars over the years, both times when his regular car was in the shop. One loaner he drove before college after he got a flat tire from driving through a construction site (Loaner A). The other loaner Martin needed during college after he parked too close to a wild fraternity party and one of his car windows was broken (Loaner B). Which of the follow correctly pairs the loaner car with the car in the shop?

(A) *Loaner A*, Buick Roadmaster. *Loaner B*, Volkswagen bug.

(B) *Loaner A*, Prius. *Loaner B*, Volkswagen bug.

(C) *Loaner A*, Prius. *Loaner B*, Buick Roadmaster

(D) *Loaner A*, Buick Roadmaster. *Loaner B*, Prius.

For 6.7 and 6.8

Marathon training plans break up the mileage in different ways. The graphic shows a list of the various training elements and their corresponding mileage.

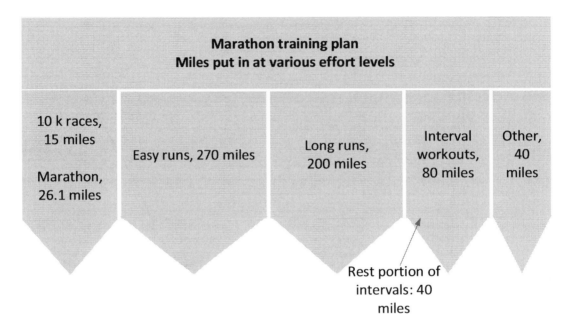

6.7 Which of the following two statements about this diagram is or are correct?

I. The training plan includes the "rest portion" of interval workouts under the broader category "interval workouts." If in another plan, rest portions were included under the "easy runs" category, then the entire "easy run" distance would be 310 miles and "interval workouts" would only be 40 miles.

II. If a small extra arrow was found at "other" for the purpose of a more exact listing of "cool downs" (which add up in mileage to 15 miles), then the category of "other" would only be 20 miles.

(A) Only statement I is correct.

(B) Only statement II is correct.

(C) Both statements are correct.

(D) Neither of the two statements is correct.

6.8 If someone were to skip half of their long runs, and instead double their interval work, how many more/fewer miles would they run in total?

(A) No change

(B) 20 more miles

(C) 20 fewer miles

(D) 60 fewer miles

6.9

Gustav Mahler was born in 1860 to Bernhard und Marie (maiden-name Herrmann) Mahler. At the age of only fifteen, he moved to Vienna and attended a conservatory while independently studying for school and university. Afterwards, he held several positions as choir-master before becoming director of the Vienna Opera in 1897 and reforming the opera in scenography. Before accepting this prestigious position, Mahler converted from Judaism to Catholicism to preempt anti-Semitic campaigns. In 1902, he married Alma Schindler, who was almost twenty years younger than him. The marriage resulted in two daughters, Maria Anna and Anna Justine, but the older daughter died suddenly in 1907. This tragedy hit the family very hard: Alma Mahler accused her husband of having caused their daughter's death by his prior composing of the *Kindertotenlieder*. Gustav mourned by writing *Das Lied von der Erde*, while Alma began an affair with the then unknown architect Walter Gropius. In 1908, Gustav Mahler moved to New York City where he conducted at the Met Opera before becoming chief conductor of the New York Philharmonic Orchestra (which was founded for him). In 1911, he died of a heart disease in Vienna. As Mahler was a conductor most of his life and only composed music on the side, he left few works be-hind. In addition to his songs, he is known for his symphonies. Although Gustav Mahler is the most famous, he was not the only one in his family with musical talent. His two sisters, Justine and Emma, were married to the brothers Arnold and Eduard Rosé. Alma Rosé, born in 1906, was Gustav Mahler's niece. She had a brother named Alfred and, like her father, she became a violinist. After a successful career, however, she had to go into hiding at to the outbreak of the Second World War because of her Jewish origin and could only give secret, illegal concerts. Unlike her father and brother (her mother had already died), Alma Rosé was unable to escape the war and was deported to Auschwitz in 1943. There, she was named director of the female orchestra and helped prevent the death of nearly all its members. However, Alma Rosé died in the camp in 1944, less than a year before its liberation.

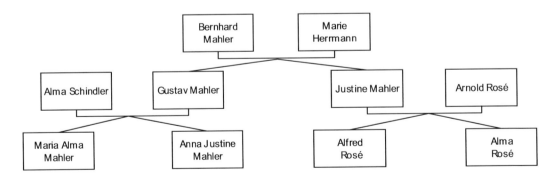

Which of the following statements is or are correct?

I. Within the family tree, the branch of Gustav Mahler and Alma Schindler is correct.

II. Within the family tree, the branch of Justine Mahler and Arnold Rosé is correct.

(A) Only statement (I) is correct.

(B) Only statement (II) is correct.

(C) Both statements are correct.

(D) Neither of the two statements is correct.

For 6.10 and 6.11

Many people are interested in understanding what makes a marriage successful. There are endless possible factors; for example, how the couple communicates, whether or not they have children, how much money they make, etc. Although no one can say with certainty what causes a successful marriage, researchers have identified certain factors which are related to a couple's chance of divorcing. People with more years of formal education tend to get married later, and couples that get married later have lower rates of divorce. However, income also plays a role. The fewer years of formal education someone has, the lower their income. But the greater a couple's income, the lower their chance of divorce. Thus, the relationship between years of formal education, income, and chance of divorce can be depicted as below.

6.10 Which of the following statements is or are correct?

   I. The relationship between years of formal education, age at marriage, income and chance of marriage success can be depicted as below:

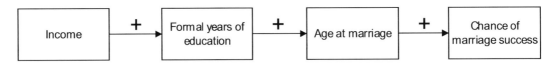

   II. The relationship between years of formal education, age at marriage, income, and chance of marriage success can be depicted as below:

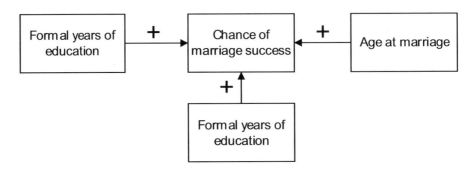

(A) Only statement (I) is correct.

(B) Only statement (II) is correct.

(C) Both statements are correct.

(D) Neither of the two statements is correct.

6.11 What is the relationship between formal years of education, income and age of marriage, and chance of marriage success?

(A)

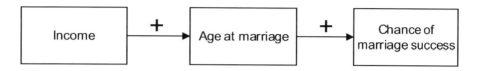

(B)

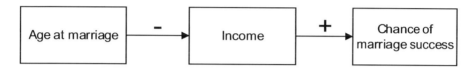

(C)

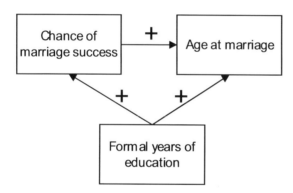

(D)

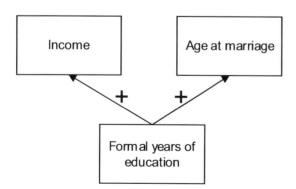

6.12

If two people who are type O blood have children, their children will also be type O. Half-siblings share one parent.

Alex has type O blood. His first wife, Mary, also has type O blood. Alex had children with Mary but has since remarried and also has children with Alice. Laura has blue eyes like her mom. George has brown hair like his dad. Sophie and Sarah are twins. Their younger brother Max has type A blood. Ben just has one full-sibling and has green eyes like his mom.

Which of the following diagrams pair the children with their biological mother?

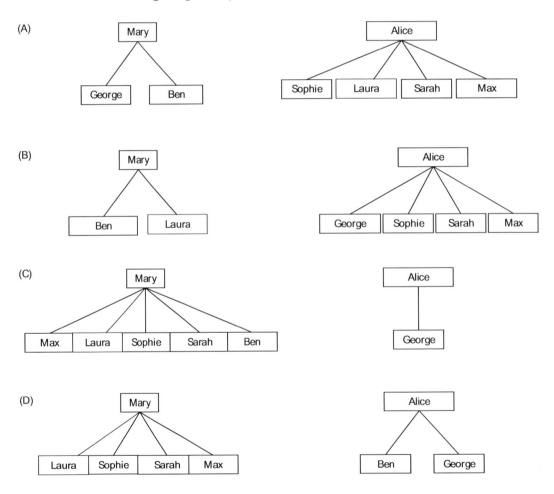

For 6.13 and 6.14

Living things can be divided into two categories: Prokaryotes and Eukaryotes. Humans are a species of Eukaryotes. Prokaryotes are subdivided into bacteria and archaea (domains). The three domains of life are Eukaryota, Bacteria, and Archaea. An example species of Bacteria is E. coli (Escherichia coli). This species is associated with causing vomiting and diarrhea, although most people don't realize that it is only a small subset of strains of E. coli that makes us sick. Most strains of E. coli are not only non-harmful, but healthy. As such, E. coli can be subdivided into the stains that make us sick (pathogenic) and the strains that don't (harmless). The strains can further be divided into serotypes. One of the most dangerous serotypes of E. coli is O157:H7. It is typically ingested through raw milk or undercooked ground beef. This serotype is a part of the larger strain STEC. Some of the other pathogenic strains are ETEC, EPEC, EAEC, EI-EC, and DAEC. Some bacteria are classified as gram positive (their phylum, a subdivision right after their domain), but E. Coli is not. E. Coli, in contrast, is in the phylum Proteobacteria. There are many other phyla under the domain of bacteria, as well as under the domains of Archaea and Eukaryotes. For example, humans (Eukaryotes) are of the Chordata phylum. Unlike bacteria, Eukaryotes are classified into kingdoms before phylum. Humans are in the Animalia kingdom.

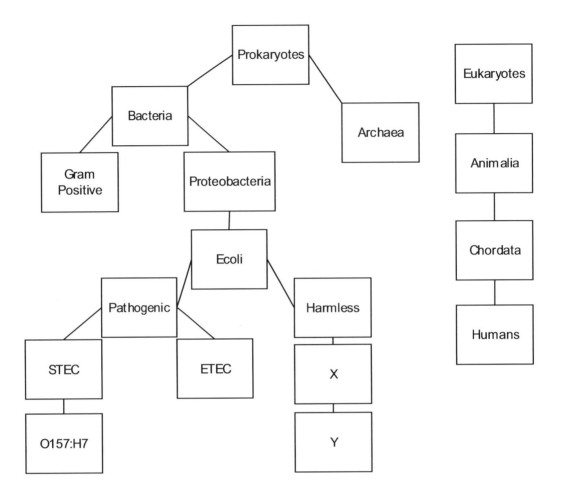

6.13 Which of the following statements is or are correct?

I.   The diagram is missing phylum, domains, strains, and serotypes which are mentioned in the text.

II. X represents a non-harmful serotype of E. Coli.

(A) Only statement (I) is correct.

(B) Only statement (II) is correct.

(C) Both statements are correct.

(D) Neither of the two statements is correct.

6.14 What phylum is EIEC?

(A) Gram Positive

(B) Chordata

(C) Bacteria

(D) Proteobacteria

6.15

The total monthly cost of the Berlin café "Waffelzeit" amounts to € 10,000. The following graphic shows how the costs are divided:

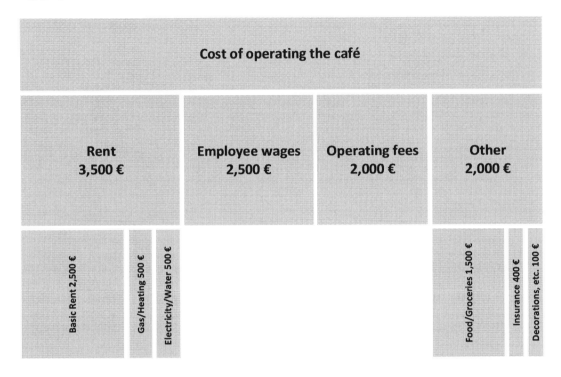

Which of the following statements is or are correct?

I.   If there were another box labeled "Vegetables € 500" below the "Groceries" box, then "Groceries would be € 2,000" and "Others € 2,500", and the total costs would increase accordingly to € 10,500.

II. In the graphic, "Insurance 400 €" is listed under "Other". If you moved this sub-item to "Rent" and added "Napkins and tablecloths 400 €" (a cost not otherwise accounted for) under "Other," "Other 2,000 €" would stay that way and "Rent" would increase to "Rent 3,900 €". The total cost would be € 10,400.

(A) Only statement (I) is correct.

(B) Only statement (II) is correct.

(C) Both statements are correct.

(D) Neither of the two statements is correct.

For 6.16 and 6.17

Gardeners in the UK know of the damage some slugs can do to their plants. The Agriolimax reticulatus is particularly common and a threat to well-kept gardens.

The more slugs in a garden, the more damage the plants will suffer (except for during periods of drought. During droughts, slugs will hide away, leaving the plants alone and refraining from mating). Gardeners can try to kill slugs with poison, and although temporarily effective, the slugs will typically repopulate by the next year.

Agriolimax reticulatus slugs can lay multiple batches of eggs from just one mating, with the first batch having the most eggs, and the number of eggs laid decreasing each batch. Most eggs are laid during the warmer months and at night time. Slugs need a moist surface to both mate and lay their eggs on. The more eggs that are laid, the more slugs that will eventually populate the garden and wreak havoc to the plants.

6.16   **Which of the following statements is or are correct regarding the following diagram?**

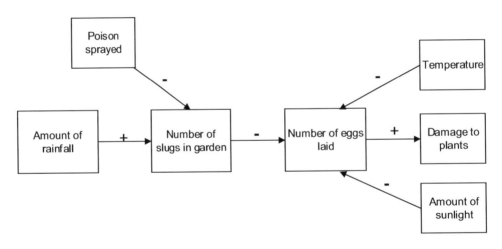

I.   The relationship depicted between temperature and amount of sunlight to the number of eggs laid is correct.

II.   The relationship depicted between poison sprayed and amount of rainfall to the number of slugs in garden is correct.

(A) Only statement (I) is correct.

(B) Only statement (II) is correct.

(C) Both statements are correct.

(D) Neither of the two statements is correct.

6.17 Suppose an invasive species of caterpillars is introduced to the UK which kills Agriolimax reticulatus. Like slugs, these caterpillars thrive in gardens, except when poison is sprayed. Poison eradicates the caterpillars completely and permanently (unlike the slugs who can return next year). How can one show these effects in a diagram?

I. The presence of caterpillars is connected to damage to plants using $\xrightarrow{-}$ and is connected to number of slugs in garden areas using $\xrightarrow{-}$.

II. Damage to plants is connected to both the presence of caterpillars and the amount of rainfall using $\xrightarrow{-}$ and is connected to number of slugs in the garden using $\xrightarrow{+}$.

(A) Only statement (I) is correct.

(B) Only statement (II) is correct.

(C) Both statements are correct.

(D) Neither of the two statements is correct.

6.18

The position of supreme ruler of China is not elected by the people, but has been held by the Communist Party's Secretary General (known as the chairman before 1980) since 1949. When the People's Republic of China was founded in 1949, Mao Zedong became China's first supreme leader. In addition to stabilization and communization of China, Mao was also responsible for the Great Leap Forward during which millions of people starved. After his death in 1976, his widow Jiang Qing tried to seize power, but was arrested and Hua Guofeng became the new chairman of the Communist Party. During this time, there was another wing within the party under Deng Xiaoping. This faction grew especially strong at the 1977 party convention and was able to assert Deng's positions: a year later, a phase of reform began, and policies were implemented to begin opening China to the west. In 1980, Hu Yaobang became Secretary General of the Communist Party (and became chairman in 1981). He was replaced by Zhao Zi-yang in 1987. After Hu Yaobang's death in 1989, there were student protests over Deng Xiaoping's imposition of martial law. These protests culminated in the Tiananmen massacre. After that, Jiang Zemin, supported by Deng Xiaoping (who still shaped the political direction of the party) became the new Secretary General. With the help of Zhu Rongji, Jiang Zemin was responsible for numerous economic reforms, and China joined the WTO in 2001, which further accelerated its opening to the West. Jiang Zemin deepened his power by taking over the position of President, which was held by Yang Shangkun, in 1993, in addition to being Secretary General. He resigned from office in 2002 and was succeeded by Hu Jintao, under whom China rose to become Asia's largest economic power. Xi Jinping finally came to power in 2012 and eventually had the term limit lifted, enabling him to remain China's top leader for life.

Which illustration shows the correct timeline of the supreme rulers of China?

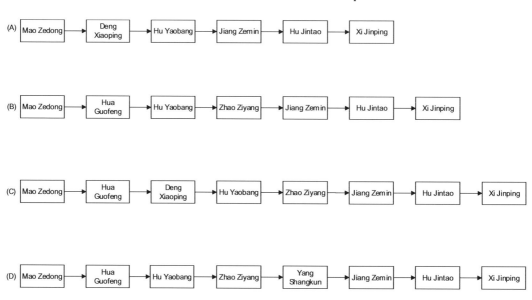

Practice test – Core Test and Humanities-, Cultural Studies and Social Sciences

For 6.19 and 6.20

Red wine contains resveratrol, an antioxidant thought to reduce the risk of cancer and vision loss. Yet red wine also contains alcohol, which increases blood pressure. Drinking less alcohol can also help with weight loss. And one way to lower blood pressure is by losing weight.

6.19 Which of the following statements is or are correct?

    I.   Red wine can contribute to weight gain, which in turn may raise blood pressure.

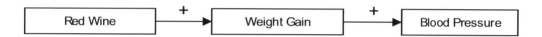

    II. If people drink more red wine when stressed, then the following diagram would be true:

    (A) Only Statement I is correct.

    (B) Only Statement II is correct.

    (C) Both statements are correct.

    (D) Neither statement is correct.

6.20 One way that drinking less wine contributes to weight loss is through exercise, such that drinking red wine contributes to decreased motivation to exercise, and exercise promotes weight loss. The relationship between weight loss, red wine, and exercise is correctly depicted in the following way?

(A) Weight loss is connected to red wine using $\xrightarrow{-}$ and is connected to exercise using $\xrightarrow{+}$.

(B) Red wine is connected to weight loss using $\xrightarrow{-}$ and is connected to exercise using $\xrightarrow{-}$.

(C) Red wine is connected to weight loss using $\xrightarrow{-}$, and exercise connects red wine to weight loss such that red wine $\xrightarrow{-}$ exercise $\xrightarrow{-}$ weight loss.

(D) Exercise is connected to red wine using $\xrightarrow{-}$ and connected to weight loss using $\xrightarrow{+}$.

6.21

Every economic system needs to develop new workforces to increase its productivity, and in the process, create more jobs. When there are too few available jobs, the un-employment rate increases, which has a negative impact on the economic system.

Which of the following statements is or are correct?

I.   Workforce is connected to the economic system through $\xrightarrow{+}$ with the arrow pointing towards the economic system.

II. Jobs are connected to productivity through $\xrightarrow{+}$ and with the economic system through $\xrightarrow{-}$. $\xrightarrow{+}$ points to jobs, and $\xrightarrow{-}$ points to economic system.

(A) Only statement (I) is correct.

(B) Only statement (II) is correct.

(C) Both statements are correct.

(D) Neither of the two statements is correct.

6.22

Caffeine, mostly ingested through coffee, has various effects on the body. In general, caffeine stimulates the metabolism: it stimulates digestion so that food is digested more quickly. The central nervous system (CNS) is also stimulated by caffeine. Stimulation of the CNS has various effects, such as making someone feel more alert and awake, as well as improving concentration. Caffeine also acts to increase the diameter of peripheral blood vessels (arteries, veins, capillaries), which means that muscles are better supplied with oxygen. However, coffee functions to decrease the diameter of vessels in the brain, which can lead to headaches.

The following illustration shows the effect of caffeine on the human body.

D = diameter of blood vessels in the brain
HA = headache
PV = peripheral vessels
O2 = oxygen
MB = stimulation of metabolism
DG = digestion

CNS = excitation central nervous system
F = fatigue
CT = concentration

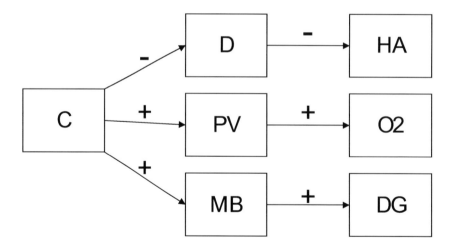

Which of the following statements is or are correct?

I. The figure can be supplemented by connecting the CNS with a $\xrightarrow{+}$ to C, and connecting both F and CT with a $\xrightarrow{+}$ to C. A $\xrightarrow{+}$ points from C to CNS and from CNS to F and CT.

II. The relationship between caffeine, diameter of the blood vessels in the brain and headache is shown correctly in the figure.

(A) Only statement (I) is correct.

(B) Only statement (II) is correct.

(C) Both statements are correct.

(D) Neither of the two statements is correct.

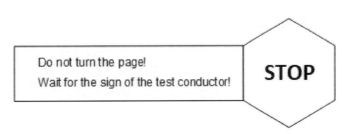
Do not turn the page!
Wait for the sign of the test conductor!

STOP

TEST MODULE: RECOGNIZING LINGUISTIC STRUCTURES

You will receive sentences in English and in various fictional languages. Now, you need to determine the rules of each of those languages and translate the sentence based on those rules. After two questions, you will receive a new fictional language that is in no way related to the fictional language from the previous questions.

During the exam, you have a total of **50 minutes** to answer the **22 questions** in the "Recognizing Linguistic Structures" section.

EXAMPLE

momle lomanozete rokoz	=	The father helps his son.
naqumi katoze talokoz	=	The mother greets the dog.
molde katozete sumolüm	=	The student hugs his dog.
ronume molde ranilüm	=	The professor likes the student.

"The professor hugs the student and her son" is expressed in the foreign language by:

(A) moldexümoldi ronume sumokoz

(B) ronume moldexütakonete sumolüm

(C) lomanozexükatoze ronume sumolüm

(D) ronume moldexütakonete ronume

Answer: B

Verb: to hug = sumolüm, possible answers: B, C.

Object: the student = molde, her son = takonete, answer: B.

Additional clues:

- *Subject: the professor = ronume*
- *and = -xü-*

FOR 7.1. AND 7.2

leötokuzy	=	I wrote
löetokö	=	he reads
leötoko	=	you (singular) write
löetokämi	=	they will read
leötokü	=	we write

7.1. **"We read and he wrote" is expressed in the foreign language by:**

(A) löetokü tomo leötoko

(B) löetoku tomo leötokozy

(C) leötokü tomo leötoko

(D) löetoküzy tomo leötoközy

7.2. **"I will read and you (singular) will write" is expressed in the foreign language by:**

(A) löetokumi tomo leötokomi

(B) leöetokumi tomo leötokomi

(C) leötoku tomo löetokomi

(D) löetoku tomo leötokomi

FOR 7.3. AND 7.4.

qalogut zo	=	I drove.
Qelogut	=	You (singular) drive.
qamopu	=	I sleep.

7.3. **"Do you (singular) go?" is expressed in the foreign language by:**

(A) tolutqe zo

(B) tolummqe

(C) toluqa maq

(D) qeloqu zo

7.4. **"I drive and you (singular) sleep" is expressed in the foreign language by:**

(A) qalogut zo qemoput

(B) qelogut zö qamopu

(C) qelogut zö qamopu

(D) qalogut zö qemopu

FOR 7.5. AND 7.6

moloztipe boto xoxiq	=	The architect draws rapidly.
lumetepi moloztipe xax	=	The painter calls the architect.
maleztipe boto xuxy	=	The intern writes rapidly.
lumeztipe maleztipe xüxlim	=	The painters annoy the intern.

7.5.   **"The architect calls the painter" is expressed in the foreign language by:**

(A) lumetepi xüxlim moloztipe

(B) moloztepi lumetipe xüxlim

(C) moloztipe lumetepi xax

(D) lumetepi molozlipe xax

7.6.   **"The intern draws the architect" is expressed in the foreign language by:**

(A) maleztipe xoxiq moloztipe

(B) maleztipe moloztipe xoxiq

(C) moloztipe xuxy maleztipe

(D) moloztipe maleztipe xuxy

lueqezülma	=	I sang
laeqekom	=	he talks
luequzülmy	=	we will sing
loequzül	=	you (plural) sing
laequkomma	=	they talked

7.7. "You (singular) talk" is expressed in the foreign language by:

(A) luequkom

(B) loequkom

(C) laeqekom

(D) loeqekom

7.8. "She will talk" is expressed in the foreign language by:

(A) laeqekommy

(B) laeqekom

(C) loeqekommy

(D) laequkom

FOR 7.9. AND 7.10

lamo pe   =   you (singular) come

lamo te   =   you (plural) come

bamo te   =   you (plural) leave

7.9. **"You (plural) will come" is expressed in the foreign language by:**

(A) xibamo te

(B) xilamo pe

(C) te xibamo

(D) xilamo te

7.10. **"You (singular) come and you (singular) stay" is expressed in the foreign language by:**

(A) lamo pe tilo gamo pe

(B) lamo pe tilo lamo pe

(C) lamo pe tilo gamote

(D) lamope tilo lamo pe

FOR 7.11. AND 7.12.

ba ?zuxöm lem	=	Will he read?
kito bao	=	She writes.
kito nep ba	=	He wrote.
?kito lem bao	=	She will write.

7.11. "Did they write?" is expressed in the foreign language by:

(A) baoz kito nep

(B) baoz kito

(C) baoz zuxöm nep

(D) ?kito lem baz

7.12. "She reads and he will write" is expressed in the foreign language by:

(A) zuxöm bao toki ?kito lem ba

(B) zuxöm bao ?toki kito lem ba

(C) zuxöm ba toki ?kito ba

(D) kito bao toki lem bam

FOR 7.13. AND 7.14

mulkamörz	=	The daughter cooks.
nemguleng tolo mörzxe	=	The father asks his daughter.
mulkugümp rak	=	The friend cooks willingly.
laczuram tolo gümpxe	=	The neighbor visits his friend.

7.13. "The daughter asks her friend" is expressed in the foreign language by:

(A) nemgamörz tolo gümpxe

(B) mulkigümp tolo mozxe

(C) nemgimorz tolo gümpxe

(D) mulkimorz tolo gümpxe

7.14. "The neighbor willingly visits his father" is expressed in the foreign language by:

(A) luczamörz rate tolo lengxe

(B) nemgigümp tolo lengxe rak

(C) laczuram rak tolo lengxe

(D) laczuram rate tolo ramxe

ko narux	=	She swims regularly.
te zynorux	=	You (singular) will swim a lot.
li zyrux	=	You (plural) will swim.
zynamot tu	=	Will I dance regularly?
lörux li	=	Do you swim often?

7.15. **"Will she swim often" is expressed in the foreign language by:**

(A) zylörux ko

(B) zylömok ko

(C) zylomole li

(D) zylöruxlö ko

7.16. **"Do you (singular) dance regularly?" is expressed in the foreign language by:**

(A) te zymotna

(B) motna te

(C) namot te

(D) namotna te

FOR 7.17. AND 7.18.

ketlinmi mule ilem	=	the woman is young
ketlomni liop kitmoil oulem	=	the man happily reads the book
ketlinmo elko ilem	=	the grandma is old
kitmoil meil ilem	=	the book is beautiful

7.17. "The man happily takes the flowers" is expressed in the foreign language by:

(A) ketlomni liop ketloimo lupi

(B) meil ilem ketloimo liop

(C) ketlomni ilem liop ketloimo

(D) liop ketlomni lupi ketloimo

7.18. "The man and the woman read the old book" is expressed in the foreign language by:

(A) ketlomni oten ketlinmi kitmoil elko oulem

(B) ketlomni oten ketlinmi oulem elko kitmoil

(C) ketlomni oten kelinmo kitmoil elko oulem

(D) ketlomni oten ketlinmi kitmoil oulem ilem

FOR 7.19. AND 7.20.

lomvelz roxalk nep	=	The cat is black.
lomnoly boking nep	=	The lawn is green.
lamvoxs peny komolx tos	=	The boy always plays soccer.
lemrasx peny minorz nep	=	The horse is always tired.

7.19. "The black horse plays on the lawn" is expressed in the foreign language by:

(A) roxalklamrasx lomnoly tos

(B) lemrasxroxalk lomnoly tos

(C) lamnoly lemrasxroxalk tos

(D) lemrasx roxalk nep lomnaly tos

7.20. "The cat and the boy are tired" is expressed in the foreign language by:

(A) neplo roxalk lomvelz lamvoxs minorz

(B) minorz leamvelz lomvoxs neplo

(C) lomvelz at lamvoxs minorz neplo

(D) lemrasx at lamvoxs minorz neplo

FOR 7.21. AND 7.22.

sosdslutelv	=	The neighbor listens to music.
pozkarnamsosd	=	The fireman finds the neighbor.
pozgorgovt	=	The fire burns in the kitchen.
pozkarspazel	=	The fireman saves the woman.

7.21. **"The fire scares the neighbor" is expressed in the foreign language by:**

(A) pozuplasosd

(B) pozkarspasosd

(C) pozspasosd

(D) sosduplapoz

7.22. **"The woman listens to music in the kitchen" is expressed in the foreign language by:**

(A) sosdslutelvgovt

(B) zelslutelvgovt

(C) zelspatelvgovt

(D) telvgovtsluzel

DETAILLED ANSWERS

3

ANSWER KEY

Solving Quantitative Problems		Inferring Relationships	
Question	Answer	Question	Answer
1.1	B	2.1	B
1.2	A	2.2	C
1.3	B	2.3	D
1.4	C	2.4	A
1.5	D	2.5	B
1.6	A	2.6	B
1.7	C	2.7	D
1.8	D	2.8	A
1.9	A	2.9	B
1.10	B	2.10	C
1.11	B	2.11	B
1.12	B	2.12	A
1.13	C	2.13	C
1.14	A	2.14	A
1.15	D	2.15	C
1.16	B	2.16	B
1.17	C	2.17	B
1.18	A	2.18	C
1.19	C	2.19	D
1.20	B	2.20	A
1.21	D	2.21	D
1.22	A	2.22	C

Completing Patterns			Continuing Numerical Series	
Question	Answer		Question	Answer
3.1	E		4.1	1029
3.2	E		4.2	-3
3.3	E		4.3	-156
3.4	D		4.4	630
3.5	D		4.5	76
3.6	F		4.6	128
3.7	D		4.7	-136
3.8	A		4.8	210
3.9	E		4.9	548
3.10	D		4.10	-10
3.11	B		4.11	8
3.12	A		4.12	-72
3.13	D		4.13	-5
3.14	B		4.14	640
3.15	D		4.15	66
3.16	D		4.16	4320
3.17	D		4.17	4
3.18	B		4.18	18
3.19	D		4.19	-72
3.20	F		4.20	3
3.21	B		4.21	3
3.22	C		4.22	150

Understanding and Interpreting Texts		Using Representation Systems Flexibly		Recognizing Linguistic Structures	
Question	Answer	Question	Answer	Question	Answer
5.1	B	6.1	D	7.1	D
5.2	A	6.2	C	7.2	A
5.3	B	6.3	D	7.3	B
5.4	A	6.4	C	7.4	A
5.5	D	6.5	C	7.5	C
5.6	A	6.6	C	7.6	B
5.7	A	6.7	A	7.7	D
5.8	D	6.8	C	7.8	A
5.9	D	6.9	B	7.9	D
5.10	B	6.10	B	7.10	A
5.11	D	6.11	D	7.11	A
5.12	A	6.12	A	7.12	A
5.13	B	6.13	D	7.13	A
5.14	A	6.14	C	7.14	C
5.15	D	6.15	B	7.15	A
5.16	A	6.16	B	7.16	C
5.17	A	6.17	A	7.17	A
5.18	A	6.18	B	7.18	A
5.19	A	6.19	C	7.19	B
5.20	D	6.20	B	7.20	C
5.21	A	6.21	A	7.21	A
5.22	A	6.22	B	7.22	B

ANSWER KEY – CONTINUING NUMERICAL SERIES

	-	0	1	2	3	4	5	6	7	8	9
01		x	x	x							x
02	x				x						
03	x		x				x	x			
04		x			x			x			
05								x	x		
06			x	x						x	
07	x		x		x			x			
08		x	x	x							
09						x	x			x	
10	x	x	x								
11										x	
12	x			x					x		
13	x						x				
14		x				x		x			
15								x			
16		x		x	x	x					
17						x					
18			x							x	
19	x			x					x		
20					x						
21					x						
22		x	x				x				

CORE TEST: SOLVING QUANTITATIVE PROBLEMS

1.1   Answer: B

Step 1: determine the scale. Scale => 35 cm : 280 km.

Step 2: Convert km to m. 35 cm : 280,000 m (1 km = 1000 m).

Step 3: Convert m to cm. 35 cm : 28,000,000 cm (1 m = 100 cm).

Step 4: solve for 1 cm. 1 cm : (28,000,000 cm / 35 cm), 1 cm : 800,000 cm.

1.2   Answer: A

Determine how many employees do the same job:

120 – 15 assistants = 105 specialist consultants and managing directors

> *x = number of managing directors*

> *4x = number of consultants*

> *x + 4x = 105 employees*

> *5x = 105 employees*

> *x = 21.*

So, there are 21 managing directors who collectively receive 21 × 20,000 = 420,000 euros in annual salary.

1.3   Answer: B

The distance between the stable and garden shed is: 23.42 m + 59.68 m = 83.1 m.

1.4 Answer: C

$$3 \triangleq 8h$$

$$5 \triangleq x$$

$$\Rightarrow \frac{3 \times 8h}{5} \approx 4.8h$$

1.5 Answer: D

If speed = distance / time, then distance = time × speed applies.

Step 1: convert the speed into meters / hour:
88 km/h × 1,000 = 88,000 m/h.

Step 2: convert the speed to meters / second:
88,000 m/h = 88,000 m / 3,600 seconds.

Step 3: Determine how many meters the taxi would cover in 2 seconds:
Distance   = 88,000 m / 3,600 s × 2 s

               = (88,000 × 2) / 3,600

               = 48.9 m.

1.6 Answer: A

Step 1: convert minutes to hours:

20 / 60 = 0.3333

Sven drove a total of 6.3333 hours.

If speed = distance / time, then distance = time × speed.

Step 2: Use the formula to solve the question:

Distance = 48 km/h × 6.3333 h = 304 km.

1.7   Answer: C

The son rides faster than his father. Calculate the time it takes the son and father to each travel 1.5 km. The difference is the time the son has to wait for the father.

Step 1: calculate how many minutes each of the two takes to cover 1.5 km:

If speed = distance / time, then time = distance / speed.

Son: 1.5 km / 30 km/h = 0.05 h

Father: 1.5 km / 15 km/h = 0.1 h

Step 2: calculate the time difference and convert it into minutes:

0.1 h – 0.05 h = 0.05 h = 0.05 × 60 min = 3 min.

1.8   Answer: D

The volume of the tank is given and is $10 \times 30 \times 20 = 6{,}000 \ m^3$. With a filling speed of 10 m^3 per minute, it takes 6.000 / 10 = 600 minutes until the tank is full. 600 minutes is the equivalent of 10 hours: 600 / 60 = 10 hours.

1.9   Answer: A

Solution by compound rule of three:

Step 1: calculate how long it will take the original 5 carpenters to tile an area of 50 m^2:

$10 \ m^2$	≙	$8 \ h$
$1 \ m^2$	≙	$8 / 10 \ h = 0.8 \ h$
$50 \ m$	≙	$0.8 \ h \times 50 = 40 \ h$

8 carpenters need 40 hours to tile an area of 50 m^2.

Step 2: calculate how long it takes 4 Carpenters to do this:

$$5\ C \quad \triangleq \quad 40\ h$$
$$1\ C \quad \triangleq \quad 40\ h \times 5 = 200\ h$$
$$4\ C \quad \triangleq \quad 200\ h\ /\ 4 = 50\ h$$

4 carpenters need 50 hours to tile an area of 50 m².

1.10 Answer: B

On a segment, a point that is twice as far from one end as the other is 1/3 the distance from one end. The points (0, -1), (1, 0), and (2, 1) are on segment AB, and they divide the segment into three intervals of equal length.

1.11 Answer: D

Step 1: Formulate an equation that represents the sales of the business in the different months.

j = revenue in January

d = revenue in December

f = revenue in February

You know from the information given:

$$j = \frac{2}{5}\ d \text{ and } f = \frac{1}{4}\ j$$

Step 2: Replace j in the second equation with $\frac{2}{5}\ d$.

Step 3: Use the values above to calculate the average revenue of January and February:

Average = sum of values / number of values.

$$Average = \frac{2}{5} + \frac{2}{5} \times \frac{1}{4} = \frac{1}{2}$$

Average January and February revenue is 1/2 of December revenue. So, December's revenue is two times the average of January and February.

1.12   Answer: B

If speed = distance / time, then distance = time × speed applies.

Step 1: convert the travel time of the two into hours:

   120 min / 60 = 2 hours.

Step 2: determine how far Ben has driven in 2 hours:

   Distance = 2 h × 14 km / h

   = 28 km.

Step 3: determine how far Georg drove in 2 hours:

   Distance = 2 h × 9 km / h

   = 18 km.

Step 4: determine the route between the two cyclists:

28 + 18 = 46.

The cyclists are 46 km apart.

1.13   Answer: C

For the first place there are 6 participants to choose from, the second place can be determined from the remaining 5, the third place from the remaining 4. So, the number of possible results is 6 × 5 × 4 = 120.

1.14   Answer: A

   40,000 € × 0.0525 = 2,100 €

1.15 Answer: D

In order to be sure that she takes at least two socks of each color out of the closet, the least favorable option must be assumed: 10 blue, 10 green and 2 red socks. So, she should take 22 socks so that she has at least one pair of socks of each color.

1.16 Answer: B

Area of triangle = ½ (base)(height)

A = ½ xy

24 = ½ (y+2) y　　　　　　　　　*(substitute 24 for area and y+2 for x)*

48 = y^2 + 2y

0 = y^2 + 2y -48

0 = (y+8) (y-6)

y + 8 = 0　　y – 6 = 0　　　*(eliminate y = -8 since it has to be a positive length)*

x = 6 + 2 = 8

Since the legs y and x of the right triangle are 6 and 8 meters long, respectively, the hypotenuse, z, must be 10 meters because 6 – 8 – 10 is a Pythagorean triple.

Alternatively, the Pythagorean theorem can also be used to solve for z, where $x^2 + y^2 = z^2$. Thus, $8^2 + 6^2 = 64 + 36 = 100 = z^2$, and $\sqrt{100} = z^2$, and $\sqrt{100} = 10$.

1.17 Answer: C

Solve with simple rule of three:

100 ml	≙	1.2 g
1 ml	≙	1.2 g / 100ml = 0.012 g/ml
175 ml	≙	0.012 g / ml × 175ml = 2.1 g

1.18   Answer: A

Determine the amount of interest.

The general interest formula is:

Z   = capital × interest rate × term

   = 4,000 × (10/100) × 1

   = 400

Rudolf pays € 400 interest after the first year.

1.19   Answer: C

Let x = Marina's age

Let y = Claudia's age

Step 1: Define two equations to describe the age of the sisters:

   Age of Marina: x, Age of Claudia: y

   x + y = 45

   y = x - 11

Step 2: solve the equation for y:

   x + (x − 11)   = 45

   2x   = 56

   x   = 28

Marina is 28 years old (Claudia is 17).

1.20 Answer: B

Step 1: determine what percentage of successful test participants were men:

   = 60% of 40%

   = 60/100 × 40/100

   = 0.240

   = 24%.

Step 2: Determine what percentage of successful test participants were women:

   = 75% of (100% – 40%)

   = 75% of 60%

   = 75/100 × 60/100

   = 0.45

   = 45%.

Step 3: Determine what percentage of participants passed the test:

   = 24% + 45%

   = 69%

69% of test participants passed the test.

1.21 Answer: D

The flower bed and the path form two concentric circles. Since the path is 3 m wide, the radius of the outer circle is 8 m + 3 m = 11 m. The area of circle can be determined using the formula: area = π(radius)2.

The area of the path can thus be found by subtracting the area of the inner circle, A1, from the area of the outer circle, A2.

A2 – A1 = π × 112 – π × 82 = 121 π – 64 π = 57 π.

1.22   Answer: A

Step 1: Make a table that shows all the hours of work Loretta does within a week.

	Mon	*Tue*	*Wed*	*Thu*	*Fri*	*Weekly wage*
Working hours	*8*	*8*	*8*	*8*	*8*	*5x*
Overtime	*3*	*1*	*2*	*1*	*0*	*(3 + 1 + 2 + 1 + 0) y = 7y*

Step 2: Calculate the average number of hours in a working week.

Average   = total hours worked / 5 days.

$$= (5x + 7y) / 5$$

$$= x + 7 / 5y$$

$$= x + 1.4y.$$

CORE TEST: INFERRING RELATIONSHIPS

2.1 Answer: B

Part-Whole-Relationship

A stove is always part of the kitchen as well as a sink is part of the bathroom.

2.2 Answer: C

Part-Whole-Relationship

The record label markets the music of the musician, and the publisher markets the books of the writer.

2.3 Answer: D

Part-Whole-Relationship

Many houses make a city, and many trees make a forest.

2.4 Answer: A

Part-Whole-Relationship

Milk is produced by a cow, and eggs are produced by a hen.

2.5 Answer: B

Synonym

"Daring" means the same as "courageous", while "calm" means the same as "quiet".

2.6   Answer: B

Opposite

"Nothing" is the opposite of "everything", and "a lot" is the opposite of "few".

2.7   Answer: D

Topic and subtopic

A trout is a fish, and a Ferrari is a car.

2.8   Answer: A

Topic and subtopic

An emerald is a gemstone, and chess is a board game.

2.9   Answer: B

Topic and subtopic

A peach is a fruit, while a hamster is an animal.

2.10   Answer: C

Topic and subtopic

"Tropical" is a type of climate. A lake is a type of body of water.

Note: Banana is a type of fruit, but these two terms are in the wrong order; the generic term is to the left of the colon. It should be banana: fruit

2.11 Answer: B

Object and place

Fish are adapted to life in the ocean, and birds are adapted to life in the sky.

2.12 Answer: A

Part-Whole-Relationship

A cork is part of a bottle, and a door is part of an entrance.

2.13 Answer: C

Object and characteristic

The night is "dark", while a leaf is oftentimes "green".

Tip: Check out the part of speech. An adjective always describes the characteristic of a thing (how is the night? dark). If both given words can be described with an adjective, this is probably the right solution.

2.14 Answer: A

Object and place

A human being walks on the earth, and a bird flies in the sky.

2.15 Answer: C

Object and function

A train is used to transport things, and ice is used for cooling.

2.16 Answer: B

Performer and act

A judge returns a verdict, and a scientist makes a discovery.

2.17 Answer: B

Verb tense

"To grab" is the present tense of "grabbed", and "to let" is the present tense of the past "let".

Tip: Although the two words presented in past tenses do not look similar to one another, they share the similarity that they are the same as their infinitives, except for the endings. Do not let yourself be influenced by the fact that the tenses of different verbs sometimes look very different.

A good example of this is: to swim → swam and to sleep → slept.

2.18 Answer: C

Verb tense

"To stand" is the infinitive of "stood". "Was" is the past tense of "to be".

2.19 Answer: D

Cause and effect

"To shout" is the cause of "heard", while "to ask" is the cause of "answered".

2.20 Answer: A

Problem and solution

Silence can be solved through talking, and the cold can be solved with a warm-up.

2.21 Answer: D

Degree of development

"Warm" is less than "hot", while "clever" is less than "brilliant".

2.22 Answer: C

Degree of development

"Unendurable" is worse than "uncomfortable". "Caring" is less helpful than "devotional".

CORE TEST: COMPLETING PATTERNS

3.1

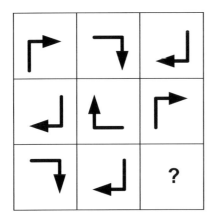

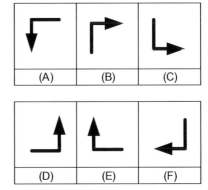

Answer: E

Direction: From left to right →

Orientation: Arrow rotates clockwise

From left to right: The arrow always rotates 90 degrees clockwise. So, there must be an arrow at the bottom right, the tip of which points to the top left.

3.2

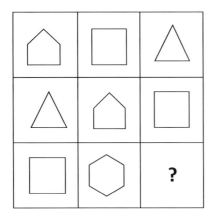 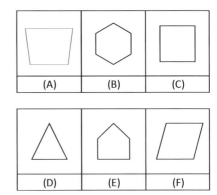

Answer: E

Direction: From left to right as well as from top to bottom → ↓

Number: The number of sides / corners in a shape does not repeat horizontally or vertically (all different).

In each row (left-right and top-bottom) the following applies: The number of lines / sides of a shape is always different. (Example, top row: number of lines 5 – 4 – 3. The middle row: 3 – 5 – 4).

The bottom-right box must have exactly 5 lines according to this rule. The bottom row has 4 – 6 –? and the right-most column has 3 – 4 –? lines. Therefore, only answer E can be correct.

3.3

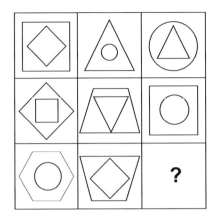 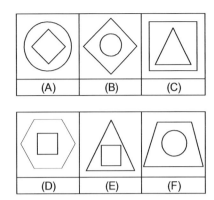

Answer: E

Direction: From left to right as well as from top to bottom →↓

Form: Outer and inner shape do not repeat (all different)

Across all rows and columns, the following applies: In none of the boxes the outer elements (or inner elements) may have an identical shape (all different).

Therefore, only the picture from answer E fits in the lower right box.

3.4

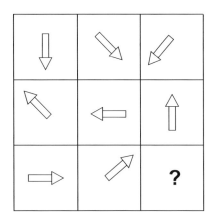

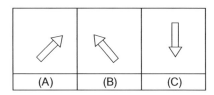

Answer: D

Direction: From left to right →

Orientation: The arrow first rotates 45° counterclockwise and then 90° clockwise.

The following applies in all rows: The arrow rotates 45° COUNTER clockwise from the 1st to the 2nd box and 90° clockwise from the 2nd to the 3rd box.

In the box on the bottom right there must be an arrow, the tip of which points to the bottom right.

3.5

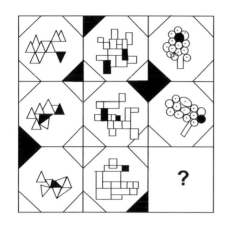

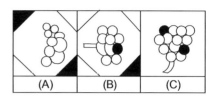

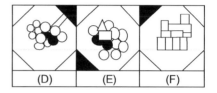

Answer: D

Direction: From top to bottom ↓

Color: 1 or 2 elements are black, outer black area rotates clockwise.

Quantity: Always one element less.

3.6

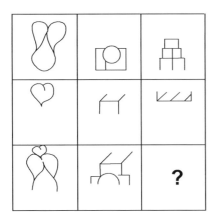

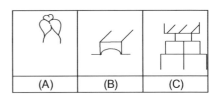

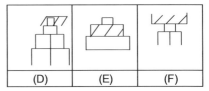

Answer: F

Direction: From top to bottom ↓

Shape: For the third image, the top two thirds of the first image are cut off and combined with the second image.

3.7

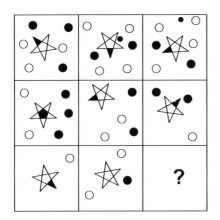

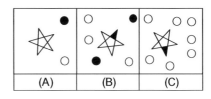

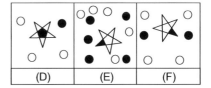

Answer: D

Direction: From top to bottom ↓

Color: The color of the star does not matter.

Quantity: The circles of the same color of the 2nd box are subtracted from the amount in the 1st box and determine the number of white and black circles of the 3rd box. The different colors are calculated separately.

3.8

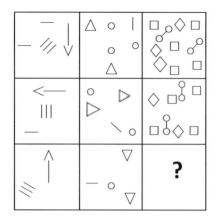

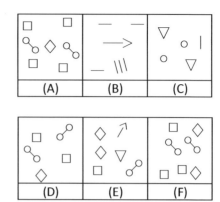

Answer: A

Direction: From top to bottom ↓

Orientation: One element is always rotated 45° counterclockwise and another 90° clockwise. All elements of a certain type are always subjected to the same change. The position of the elements doesn't matter.

Quantity: The number of a certain shape decreases by one in each step.

3.9

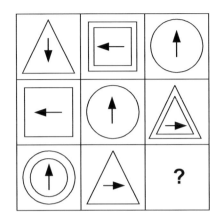 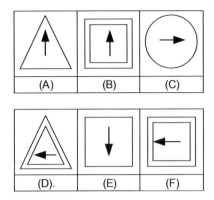

Answer: E

Direction: From left to right as well as from top to bottom →↓

Shape: Triangle, square, circle (all different); one shape each with an arrow inside

The arrows always turn (left-right and top-bottom) 90 degrees clockwise. In the bottom-right box, the arrow must point down.

3.10

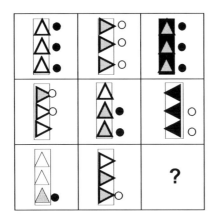 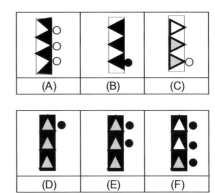

Answer: D

Direction: From left to right as well as from top to bottom →↓

Shape/Orientation: The shape and orientation of the first box is taken up again in the third box.

Quantity: horizontal → same number of dots, vertical → 3 – 2 – 1 dots.

3.11

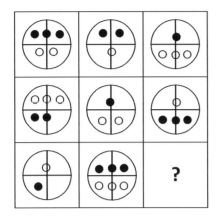
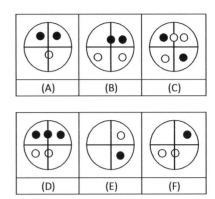

Answer: B

Direction: From left to right as well as from top to bottom →↓

Quantity: No matter whether you move across rows or down columns, there is always one (and only one) box with: one black dot, two black dots, three black dots. The same applies to the white dots. Consequently, the unknown box needs to have two white dots and two black dots. The order is not relevant.

3.12

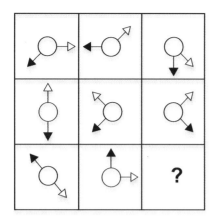

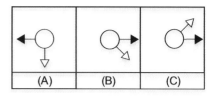

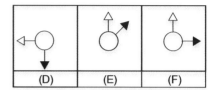

Answer: A

Direction: From left to right →

Orientation: White arrow rotates 45° counterclockwise and then 90° clockwise; black arrow rotates 45° clockwise and then 90° counterclockwise.

3.13

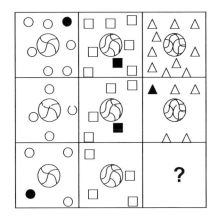

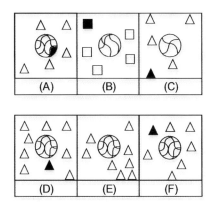

Answer: D

Direction: From top to bottom ↓

Color: In each column there are two boxes with a black element and a box without a black element. The order is irrelevant.

Quantity: Outer elements: If elements in the 1st and 2nd box overlap, they will be removed. And there is always a new element in the bottom squares.

The circular shape remains the same.

3.14

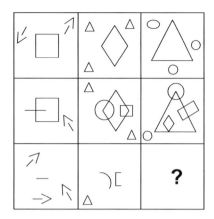

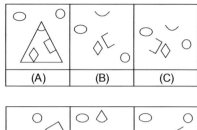

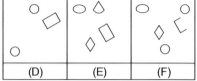

Answer: B

Direction: From top to bottom ↓

Shape: The shape of the outer elements remains the same in every column (even if the quantity differs). Apart from the outer elements, the only elements (or parts of the elements) in the third box are those that overlap with the central element in the second box; the central element and the non-overlapping parts of the smaller elements are not displayed.

Quantity: Outer elements 1 – 2 – 3 (order irrelevant).

3.15

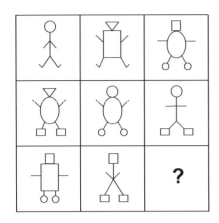

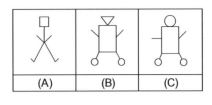

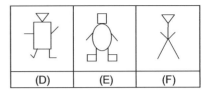

Answer: D

Direction: From top to bottom ↓

Shape: The shapes of the body, head and feet must not be repeated (head: circle, triangle, rectangle; body: line, oval, rectangle; feet: lines, rectangles, circles).

3.16

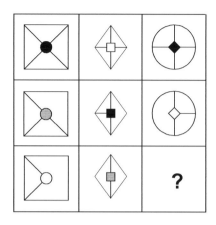

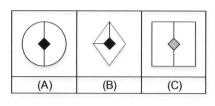

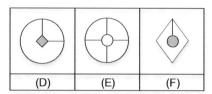

Answer: D

Direction: From top to bottom ↓

Shape: One of the inner lines is always subtracted. The outer shape in each column remains unchanged.

Color: Inner element black, white, gray (all different).

3.17

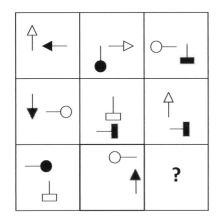
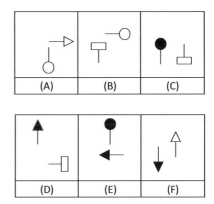

Answer: D

Direction: From top to bottom ↓

Shape: -

Orientation: The line with the black end moves 90° COUNTER clockwise. The line with the white end moves 90° clockwise.

Color: 1 × black and 1 × white per box.

3.18

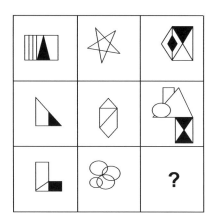

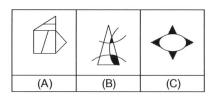

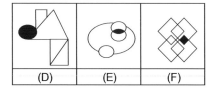

Answer: B

Direction: From top to bottom ↓

Color: The same number of elements are always black: 1 – 0 – 2 elements.

Quantity: Only the number of colored elements is decisive.

From top to bottom: The number of black elements must always remain the same. So, there must be an object with 2 black areas at the bottom right.

3.19

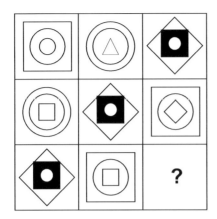

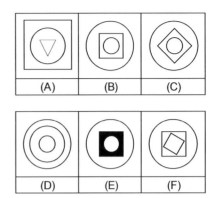

Answer: D

Direction: From left to right as well as from top to bottom →↓

Shape: Outer shapes: circle, square and rhombus (all different); middle shape: two circles and one square; the inner shape is not relevant.

Color: Two white and one black.

The bottom-right box must, therefore, have an outer circle and a middle circle.

3.20

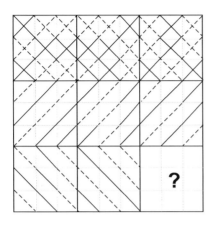

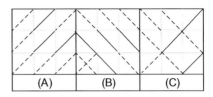

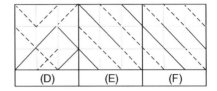

Answer: F

Direction: from left to right →

Shape: Two different line types (dashed or solid).

Orientation: Every ninth of a square moves counterclockwise.

A graphic explanation can be found below.

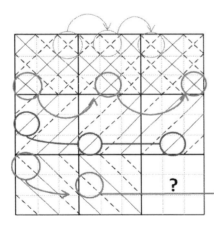

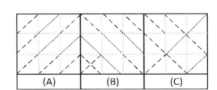

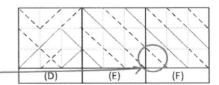

3.21

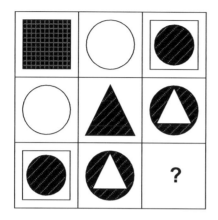

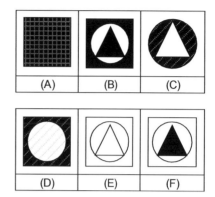

Answer: B

Direction: From left to right

Shape: 1st box + 2nd box = 3rd box (1st box become outer shape, 2nd box inner)

Color: In the 3rd box, the colors of the 1st and 2nd boxes are exchanged. If the object was previously dark, it is now light or white; if it was previously light, it is now dark or black.

In the bottom right box, there must be a dark triangle in a white circle, which in turn is completely surrounded by a dark square.

3.22

Answer: C

Direction: from top to bottom ↓

Quantity: Each box (1/9 of entire square) consists of 9 smaller boxes, each with a different number of small dots. Between the larger boxes: From row 1 to row 2 the number of dots per small box increases by 2. From row 2 to row 3 the number of dots decreases by 3. Thus, from row 1 to row 3 within each of the 9 larger boxes the number of dots decreases by 1.

3	5	4
2	4	5
4	3	3
3+2	7	4+2
2+2	6	5+2
4+2	5	3+2
5-3	4	6-3
4-3	3	7-3
6-3	2	5-3

So only answer C can be correct in the unknown box.

CORE TEST: CONTINUING NUMERICAL SERIES

4.1   126   252   255   510   513   1026   ?

Answer: 1029

The rule for this numerical series: $\times 2$ $+ 3$ $\times 2$ $+ 3$ $\times 2$ $+ 3$

4.2   −9   −6   −7   −4   −5   −2   ?

Answer: −3

The rule for this numerical series: $+ 3$ $- 1$ $+ 3$ $- 1$ $+ 3$ $- 1$

4.3   −23   −21   −42   −40   −80   −78   ?

Answer: −156

The rule for this numerical series: $+ 2$ $\times 2$ $+ 2$ $\times 2$ $+ 2$ $\times 2$

4.4   10   11   22   25   100   105   ?

Answer: 630

The rule for this numerical series: $+ 1$ $\times 2$ $+ 3$ $\times 4$ $+ 5$ $\times 6$

4.5   34   39   41   46   55   60   ?

Answer: 76

The rule for this numerical series: $+ 5$ $+ 2$ $+ 5$ $+ 9$ $+ 5$ $+ 16$

$= 2$ $= 2 + 7$ $= 9 + 7$

4.6   56   63   72   83   96   111   ?

Answer: 128

The rule for this numerical series: + 7   + 9   + 11   + 13   + 15   + 17

4.7   −112   −96   −121   −105   −129   −113   ?

Answer: −136

The rule for this numerical series: − 9   − 9   − 8   − 8   − 7

The sequence is easy to solve once you have figured out the numbers in the sequence between which relationships exist. In this case, the 1st number is related to the 3rd number, the 2nd number to the 4th number, the 3rd to the 5th, and so on.

4.8   234   236   221   225   213   219   ?

Answer: 210

The rule for this numerical series: + 2   − 15   + 4   − 12   + 6   − 9

4.9   20   11   44   36   144   137   ?

Answer: 548

The rule for this numerical series: − 9   × 4   − 8   × 4   − 7   × 4

4.10   50   45   30   25   10   5   ?

Answer: −10

The rule for this numerical series: − 5   − 15   − 5   − 15   − 5   − 15

4.11   78   76   38   36   18   16   ?

Answer: 8

The rule for this numerical series: − 2   / 2   − 2   / 2   − 2   / 2

4.12   −81   −82   −79   −80   −76   −77   ?

Answer: −72

The rule for this numerical series: − 1   + 3   − 1   + 4   − 1   + 5

4.13   −280   −140   −135   −45   −40   −10   ?

Answer: −5

The rule for this numerical series: / 2   + 5   / 3   + 5   / 4   + 5

4.14   660   670   680   650   660   670   ?

Answer: 640

The rule for this numerical series: + 10   + 10   - 30   + 10   + 10   - 30

4.15   25   32   30   30   36   33   ?

Answer: 66

The rule for this numerical series: + 7   − 2   × 1   + 6   − 3   × 2

4.16   6   6   12   36   144   720   ?

Answer: 4320

The rule for this numerical series: × 1   × 2   × 3   × 4   × 5   × 6

4.17   12   8   56   8   4   28   ?

Answer: 4

The rule for this numerical series: -4 $\times 7$ $/7$ -4 $\times 7$ $/7$

4.18   11   8   24   27   9   6   ?

Answer: 18

The rule for this numerical series: -3 $\times 3$ $+3$ $/3$ -3 $\times 3$

4.19   −27   −30   −15   −45   −48   −24   ?

Answer: −72

The rule for this numerical series: -3 $/2$ $x\,3$ -3 $/2$ $\times 3$

4.20   108   112   28   32   8   12   ?

Answer: 3

The rule for this numerical series: $+4$ $/4$ $+4$ $/4$ $+4$ $/4$

4.21   −15   −12   −9   −6   −3   0   ?

Answer: 3

The rule for this numerical series: $+3$ $+3$ $+3$ $+3$ $+3$ $+3$

4.22   80   40   36   108   54   50   ?

Answer: 150

The rule for this numerical series: $/2$ -4 $\times 3$ $/2$ -4 $\times 3$

TEST MODULE: UNDERSTANDING AND INTERPRETING TEXTS

5.1. Answer: B

Statement I is incorrect. The text states that while the first official games are often listed as having taken place in 776 BC, "many scholars (= experts) believe that the games had actually been happening in some form for many years before that."

To reach a conclusion about statement II, we must consider the final sentence ("The Olympic tradition was revived in the 1800s and the first modern games were held in 1896") in connection with the previous sentence about Theodosius I abolishing the games in AD 393. It is obvious that there are more than one thousand years between the year AD 393 and the holding of the first modern games in AD 1896. Hence, statement II is correct.

5.2. Answer: A

Statement I is correct – we know that the games had a religious element from the part of the text that says, "As well as being a sporting event, the Ancient Olympics also featured many ceremonies and ritual sacrifices to honor the god Zeus."

However, there is no information in the text to support statement II. Thus, even though we might suspect it to be true based on what we know about the modern-day Olympics, we have to conclude that – according to the text – statement II is incorrect.

5.3. Answer: B

Statement I is incorrect. Even though it may be true that environmental protection is considered an issue of secondary importance in liberal societies, the text gives no indication of this.

Statement II is clearly communicated by the text.

5.4. Answer: A

The third theory states that we all are part of society, which means that Angela Merkel is included. Therefore, statement I is correct.

However, statement II is incorrect since the text does not contain any information as to whether the FDP received the worst result in the party's history, it only states what percentage of the vote the FDP received.

5.5. Answer: D

Statement I is designed to test your attention to detail. Those of you who read the text closely should have noticed that it mentioned "a recent assessment of European wild bee species" rather than wild bee species worldwide. This means that statement I is incorrect.

As for statement II, while the text does mention that fishing practices are an issue and that many species of fish are at risk, we do not have enough information to say with certainty that statement II is correct. While it would be natural to assume some connection between fishing and endangered fish species, the text gives us no reason to suspect that fishing practices are solely responsible. Other man-made problems (such as a climate change, pollution and habitat loss) could easily be playing a role as well, and some endangered species of fish might not be valued as food at all. In light of all this, we must conclude that statement II is incorrect.

5.6. Answer: A

Statement I is correct, since the text tells us that "of all the ways that humans are changing the planet, temperature increases due to global warming are thought to be the most dangerous."

Statement II, however, is incorrect, since the text states that "if the planet warms by an average of 3 degrees Celsius, scientists predict that 8.5% of the world's species will be in danger of ceasing to exist". It tells us that there is a risk of 8.5% of the world's animal species becoming extinct, but it does not say for sure that this will happen.

5.7. Answer: A

Statement I is correct. We know this from the part of the text that says, "Without realizing what he was doing, the mouse ran over the lion, tickled him and woke him up." This conveys clearly that the mouse ran over the lion by accident, not intentionally.

Statement II is incorrect. To reach this conclusion, we must look at the part of the text that says: "He didn't see how such a small creature could ever be of any use to a lion, but he was so amused by the mouse's request that he let him go." The first part of this sentence communicates clearly that the lion didn't believe the mouse would ever be able to repay him, but that he chose to let him go anyway. The second part of the sentence tells us why – because he found the mouse's request amusing.

5.8. Answer: D

Here, our job is to identify whether these statements are explicitly given as facts in the text. Although both of them seem very likely after reading the text, we cannot say for sure – based on the information we have – that either statement can definitely be deduced.

In the case of statement I, the lion might have found another way to free himself, or the hunters might have decided to give him to a zoo, etc.

With regard to statement II, we know that the lion is happy about the mouse saving him, but this is not sufficient to guarantee that the lion will never see the mouse as prey again.

For these reasons, we have to come to the conclusion that both statements are incorrect, hence Answer D has to be selected.

5.9. Answer: D

Statement I is incorrect. While the text did state that the study's results were partially comprised of problem-focused interviews, the proportion of the study that was accounted for by the interviews is not made clear to us.

Statement II is incorrect, since the text indicates that the category system is based on qualitative content analysis, not the other way around.

5.10. Answer: B

Statement I is incorrect, since the purpose of qualitative content analysis is the systematic processing of communication content.

Statement II is correct, since according to the text, qualitative content analysis also looks at formal aspects and latent meaning.

5.11. Answer: D

Statement I is incorrect, since the last sentence of the text makes clear that David finds it difficult to take advantage of his musical (= artistic, creative) talents.

Statement II is also incorrect, because David tends to use visual means to help him remember things. No mention is made of hearing things.

5.12. Answer: A

Statement I is correct, since the text states that David is always quiet during German lessons but tends to chat with his fellow students during natural history.

Statement II is incorrect. The text makes clear that David is especially interested in the central nervous system. However, the text does not say that David really knows what the central nervous system is.

5.13. Answer: B

Statement I is incorrect since the text states that the pictures are a good three by two meters large.

Statement II is correct: "Nothing can be seen of the city, just the river Chao Phraya which (…) carries filth: pollution – the waste of civilizations. "

5.14. Answer: A

Statement I is correct: "streaks or mosaics of light, (…) amorphous spots appearing to fly. "

Statement II is incorrect: "Bangkok cannot be seen in "Bangkok"."

5.15. Answer: D

Statement I is incorrect, since banks are not the main subject of discussion.

Statement II is also incorrect, since the text explicitly states that it is questionable whether the market economy promotes moral values.

5.16. Answer: A

Statement I is correct, since the text highlights the issues but does not formulate any concrete suggestions for solving them.

Statement II is incorrect, because the text also addresses the actions of employees within a company.

5.17. Answer: A

Statement I is correct: Friedrich Ludwig Jahn, who later became the "father of gymnastics", built a sports field for gymnastics in Hasenheide in 1811. Schulke answers the question whether it can be described as an outdoor gym affirmatively.

Statement II is incorrect. The motto of the French revolution "Liberty, Equality, Fraternity" was lived there and not the German approach.

5.18. Answer: A

Statement I is correct: "The motto of the French revolution "Liberty, Equality, Fraternity" was lived here and led to the then completely new construct of a "club."

Statement II is incorrect: "Jahn was a democrat, an educated pedagogue and, to the extent military, that he was a representative of military training, but only in accordance with a war of protection, not a war of attack. "

5.19. Answer: A

The text says that the renovation has contributed to the impact of the school. Therefore, statement I is correct.

Statement II is incorrect, for it cannot be inferred from the text without a doubt. Demand is high, but the reason for this is not given.

5.20. Answer: D

Statement I is incorrect because the text does not make it clear that the premises have become large as a result of the renovation. Rather, it is possible that they were large before.

Statement II is incorrect: the school is decorated creatively, but the text does not explicitly state that the school has a creative teaching program.

5.21. Answer: A

The part of the text that states that "newspapers are faced with rising production costs (...)" clearly shows that the costs for the production (= printing) of newspapers are partially responsible for the decline in the industry. Statement I is therefore correct.

Statement II is incorrect because the text speaks of "a number of newspaper professionals". It therefore didn't speak of "most" professionals.

5.22. Answer: A

Statement I is correct. We know this from the text section "Around 350 newspapers in the United States have stopped operating." In order to draw the correct conclusion, we have to recognize that "have stopped operating" is a synonym for "going bankrupt." We also need to recognize that "over 300" could potentially mean "around 350."

Statement II is incorrect since the text states that print advertising revenue in 2014 was "the lowest since the "Newspaper Association of America" began col-

lecting industry data in 1950". This means that earnings may have been lower before, as there is no data for these years. We must therefore conclude that Statement II cannot be derived from the text.

TEST MODULE: USING REPRESENTATION SYSTEMS FLEXIBLY

6.1   Answer: D

Statement I: Germany must be at the end (and not between the Ottoman Empire and Italy), as Bremen opened its coffee houses last. The Augsburg physician only brought back stories of coffee; he did not bring the actual drink back with him to Europe. The text only tells us that the first coffee house in Europe was in Venice, so Venice should be the first European country listed. Statement I is therefore incorrect.

Statement II: For the reasons mentioned above, Augsburg must be removed from the list, as we have no information regarding the distribution of coffee in Augsburg (we only know about someone from Augsburg tasting it while abroad). Statement II is incorrect.

6.2   Answer: C

Statement I is correct: wresting is mentioned but not found in the graph.

Statement II is also correct: field hockey is at the same time as volleyball, not at the same time as lacrosse.

6.3   Answer: D

The passage tells us that Tommy competes on the cross-country team. This rules out answer C which does not mention cross country. The passage also states that the track team is an all-girls team, but Tommy is Elizabeth's boyfriend (and thus is a boy). Therefore, Tommy cannot compete in track. This rules out A and B. Answer D is the only possible answer.

6.4   Answer: C

From a careful read of the text, you see that Golden Yunnan is a black tea ("the Golden Yunnan: grown on Mango Flower Island, this black tea's..."). Answer choices A and B can therefore be eliminated. Gunpowder tea is green ("the

Gunpowder tea…it is green"). This eliminates choice D, leaving C as the correct option.

6.5   Answer: C

The passage tells us that the Buick Roadmaster is driven twice, once as the very first car ("the car he learned to drive in"), and again in college. This eliminates answer choices B and D which only list the Buick Roadmaster once. The passage states that the Prius was driven before the Volkswagen Bug, eliminating answer choice A. The correct answer is thus option C.

6.6   Answer: C

Options A and B are incorrect because the passage tells us that Martin got the Volkswagen bug before college, but the prompt tells us that Loaner B was driven during college. Option D is similarly incorrect because Martin had the Prius before he had the Volkswagen bug, which he took with him to college (i.e., he had the Prius before college). So, Loaner B can't be paired with the Prius, either. This leaves option C as correct.

6.7   Answer: A

Indeed, the amounts would be 310 miles for easy runs and 40 miles for intervals if "rest portion" switched from the "interval workouts" category to the "easy run" category. Statement I is therefore correct.

A more detailed listing would mean no change in the amount of the "other" category as a whole. For this reason, "other" is still 40 miles and statement II is incorrect.

6.8   Answer: C

If someone skips half of their long runs, they would run 100 fewer miles (200/2 = 100). But if they doubled their interval work, they would run 80 miles more. The difference is 20 miles (-100+80 = -20). In total, this would mean they run 20 fewer miles (option C).

6.9 Answer: B

Statement I: This branch is not correct. The first-born daughter's name is Maria Anna, not Maria Alma (as in the figure). Therefore, statement I is incorrect.

Statement II: This branch is correct. Justin Mahler and Arnold Rosé are married and have two children: Alfred and Alma. Statement II is correct.

6.10 Answer: B

Statement I is incorrect because the passage says nothing about income contributing to more years of education, only the reverse relationship is described.

Statement II is correct. The passage explains that the more years of formal education, the later someone gets married (+). Similarly, the more years of formal education, the greater one's in-come (+). Income and age at marriage both increase chance of marriage success (+). This means that years of education is related to greater chance of marriage success (+) through a greater age of marriage and a greater income.

6.11 Answer: D

Option A incorrectly assumes that income contributes to age at marriage

Option B suggest that the later one marries, the less their income. There is nothing in the passage to suggest this.

Option C has the relationship between age of marriage and marriage success reversed (the arrow should be pointing the other direction).

Option D is correct, as more formal education is related to greater income and a greater age at marriage. This is clarified in the passage.

6.12 Answer: A

Because Max has type A blood, Mary cannot be his mother. We know that Sophie, Sarah, and Max are siblings. Therefore, Alice is the mother of Max, Sarah, and Sophie. Ben has just one sibling; he cannot be the full-brother of Sophie, Sarah, and Max. Ben has green eyes like his mom, and Laura has blue eyes like her mom: They cannot be siblings. George must therefore be Ben's only sibling, and Laura must be the sister to Sophie, Sarah, and Max.

6.13 Answer: D

Statement I. This statement is incorrect because all of the domains of life are listed.

Statement II. This statement is incorrect because X is where the strain would be, not the serotype.

6.14 Answer: C

EIEC is a strain of E. Coli. It is stated in the passage that E. Coli is of the phylum Proteobacteria, so EIEC must be of the phylum Proteobacteria.

6.15 Answer: B

Statement I: "Vegetables" would be a subcategory of "groceries", i.e., it represents a portion of the cost of groceries, offering more detail about the cost, but not changing the actual total amount. Therefore, the cost of "food" would not increase, but would remain the same. Statement I is therefore incorrect.

Statement II: Since the cost of "insurance" and "napkins and tablecloths" are both € 400, the amount of "other" would remain the same. However, since "rent" now includes a subcategory whose costs were not before accounted for, you have to add the costs of the new subcategory, "insurance," to the existing costs in the category "rent." € 2,500 + € 500 + € 500 + € 400 = € 3,900. The total cost is calculated as follows: € 3,900 + € 2,500 + € 2,000 + € 2,000 = € 10,400. Statement II is correct.

6.16 Answer: B

Statement I is incorrect: The passage states that more eggs are laid during warmer months. This means that the higher the temperature, the more the eggs:

temperature $\xrightarrow{+}$ eggs. The relationship between amount of sunlight and number of eggs laid is correct, as eggs are laid at night. Less sunlight means more eggs laid: amount of sunlight $\xrightarrow{-}$ number of eggs laid.

Statement II is correct. The passage states that slugs hide away during a drought, meaning that the more rain there is, the more slugs that will be in the garden: amount of rainfall $\xrightarrow{+}$ amount of slugs. The passage also tells us that poison, although only temporarily, reduces the number of slugs in the garden: poison sprayed $\xrightarrow{-}$ number of slugs.

6.17 Answer: A

Statement I is correct. The prompt tells us that the more caterpillars, the fewer the slugs (caterpillars $\xrightarrow{-}$ slugs). From the passage, we know that fewer slugs leads to less damage to plants (number of slugs $\xrightarrow{+}$ damage to plants). So, when more caterpillars, there is less damage to plants: caterpillars $\xrightarrow{-}$ damage to plants.

Statement II is incorrect. The arrow connecting damage to plants and presence of caterpillars and amount of rainfall is backwards (pointing in the wrong direction). It mistakenly suggests that damage to plants causes fewer caterpillars and less rainfall. The arrow connecting damage to plants and number of slugs is also backwards/ pointed in the wrong direction. Although the arrows in Statement II have the correct sign (plus or minus), they confuse causality. As our outcome is damage to plants, the arrows should point towards (not from) damage to plants.

6.18 Answer: B

Deng Xiaoping was never the chairman or Secretary General of the Communist Party, he only "shaped the political direction of the party" for some time. Therefore, we can rule out answers A and C. Answer D is wrong because Yang Shangkun was only the President but never the Secretary General (Chairman). So, answer B is correct.

6.19 Answer: C

Statement I is correct because drinking less wine can contribute to weight loss (less to less means a positive relationship: red wine $\xrightarrow{+}$ weight gain) and *losing weight lowers blood pressure (again less to less translates to more to more; weight gain* $\xrightarrow{+}$ *blood pressure).*

Statement II is correct. Stress leads to more red wine, $\xrightarrow{+}$*, and red wine may reduce the risk of cancer,* $\xrightarrow{-}$*.*

6.20 Answer: B

Option A has the relationships reversed (the arrow is facing the wrong direction). Red wine is connected to weight loss using $\xrightarrow{-}$*, and exercise is connected to weight loss using* $\xrightarrow{+}$*, but not the other way around. Option B has this correct, and also correctly depicts the relationship between red wine and exercise: As drinking red wine decreases motivation to exercise, red wine* $\xrightarrow{-}$ *exercise. Option C is incorrect because exercise promotes weight loss, meaning exercise* $\xrightarrow{+}$ *weight loss. Finally, option D has the relationship between exercise and red wine reversed (arrow facing wrong direction); we do not know that exercising causes someone to drink less wine, we only know that drinking wine can decrease motivation to exercise.*

6.21 Answer: A

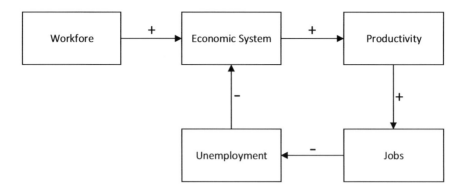

Statement I: As the workforce increases, the economic system also grows. Therefore, workers $\xrightarrow{+}$ economic system. Statement I is correct.

Statement II: The first arrow is correct, as when productivity increases there are more jobs. The second arrow is wrong because the unemployment rate has been left out of the relationship. If you leave out the unemployment rate, a positive arrow would have to be between jobs and the economic system. Therefore, statement II is incorrect.

6.22 Answer: B

Statement I: It is correct that with more caffeine, the CNS is stimulated more. When the CNS is stimulated, concentration increases. However, fatigue decreases, so there should be a $\xrightarrow{-}$ between the CNS and fatigue. Statement I is incorrect.

Statement II: With more caffeine, the diameter of the blood vessels in the brain becomes smaller. As the vessels get smaller, the chance of headache increases. Both relationships are shown correctly. Statement II is therefore correct.

TEST MODULE: RECOGNIZING LINGUISTIC STRUCTURES

7.1. Answer: D

Verb: to read, to write = löeto, leöto, possible answers: A, B, D

Personal pronouns: we, he = kü, kö, answer: D

Tense: past (-zy) and present, answer: D

Others: and = tomo

7.2. Answer: A

Verb: to read, to write = löeto, leöto, possible answers: A, D

Personal pronouns: me, you = ku, ko, possible answers: A, B

Tense: future (-mi), answer: A

Other: and =tomo

7.3. Answer: B

Personal pronoun: you (singular) = qe, possible answers: A, B.

Tense: present tense. The word zo, which indicates the past tense, should not occur in this sentence. The correct answer is B.

Additional clue:

Verb: to go = tolumm-

7.4. Answer: A

Personal pronoun & verb: I drive = qalogut; you (singular) sleep = qemopu, possible answers: A, D.

Tense: present tense. The word zo, which indicates the past tense, should not occur in this sentence. The correct answer is A.

Additional clue:

and = zö

7.5. Answer: C

Subject: the architect = moloztipe (see the repeating words in the first and the third sentence), possible answers: A, C.

Sentence structure: The subject is found at the beginning of the sentence. (To find this out, compare where "moloztipe" is in the first and the third sentence.) The correct answer is C.

Additional clues:

Verb: to call = xax. (We compare the second sentence with the answer choices and look for repetitions.)
The verb is at the end of the sentence.
Object: the painter = lumetepi

7.6. Answer: B

Subject: the intern = maleztipe, possible answers: A, B, C, D.

Sentence structure: The subject is at the beginning of the sentence. Possible answers: A, B

Verb: to draw = xoxiq. The verb is at the end of the sentence. Answer: B

7.7. Answer D

Verb: to speak = kom, possible answers: A, B, C, D

Personal pronoun: you (singular) = loeqe, answer: D

Tense: Present, answer: D

7.8. Answer: A

Verb: to speak = kom, possible answers: A, B, C, D

Personal pronoun: she/ he = laeqe, possible answers: A, B

Tense: future (-my), answer: A

7.9. Answer: D

Verb: to come = lamo, possible answers: B, D

Personal pronoun: you (plural) = te, answer: D

Tense: future (xi-), answer: D

7.10. Answer A

Verb: to come, to stay = lamo, gamo, possible answers: A, C

Personal pronouns: you (singular) = pe, answer: A

Tense: present, answer: A

Others: and = tilo

7.11. Answer: A

Verb: to write = kito, possible answers: A, B, D

Tense: past tense = nep (compare second and third sentence), answer: A.

Additional clues:

they = baoz

Sentence structure in case of a question: The sentence starts with the subject: subject → (?) + verb → tense.

7.12. Answer: A

Personal pronoun & verb: she reads = zuxöm bao, possible answers: A, B.

Tense: future tense = the symbol "?" precedes the verb and "lem" follows the verb. This means: he will write = ?kito lem ba. The answer is A.

Additional clue:

and = toki. (We can only conclude this after determining that A is the answer.)

7.13. Answer: A

Verb: to ask = nemg, possible answers: A, C

Object: her friend = tolo gümp, possible answers: A, C

Subject: the daughter = amörz (female = a), answer: A

Tense: present, answer: A

7.14. Answer: C

Verb: to visit = laczu, possible answers: C, D

Object: his father = tolo leng-xe, answer: C

Subject: the neighbor = ram, answer: C

Tense: present, answer: C

Others: willingly = rak

7.15. Answer: A

Verb: to swim = rux, possible answers: A, D

Personal pronoun: she = ko, possible answers: A, D

Tense: future (zy-), possible answers: A, D

Others: often = -lö-, answer: A

Question: personal pronoun and verb are vice versa

7.16. Answer: C

Verb: to dance = mot, possible answers: A, B, C, D

Personal pronoun: you (singular) = te, possible answers: A, B, C, D

Tense: present, possible answers t: A, B, C, D

Others: regularly = na-, answer: C

Question: personal pronoun and verb are vice versa

7.17. Answer: A

Verb: to take = lupi, possible answers: A, D

Object: the flower = ketloimo, possible answers: A, D

Subject: der Mann = ketlomni, possible answers: A, D

Personal pronoun: -

Tense: present, possible answers: A, D

Others: happily = liop

You can see from the examples that the verb is always at the end of the sentence. Answer: A.

7.18. Answer: A

Verb: to read = oulem, possible answers: A, C, D

Adjective: old = elko, possible answers: A, C

Object: the book = kitmoil, possible answers: A, C

Subject: the man, the woman = ketlomni, ketlinmi, answer: A

Tense: present, answer: A

Others: You can see from the examples that the verb is always at the end of the sentence.

7.19. Answer: B

Verb:

to play = tos, possible answers: A, B, C, D.

nep = is, "is" as verb is not asked in this sentence and additionally verbs are at the end of the sentence in this language. The answer choice D can be eliminated. Possible answers: A, B, C.

Adjective: black = -roxalk, possible answers: A, B, C.

Subject: the horse = lemrasx-, possible answers: B, C.

Object: the lawn = lomnoly, answer: B.

7.20. Answer: C

Verb: are = neplo, possible answers: A, B, C, D.

Adjective: tired = minorz, possible answers: A, B, C, D.

Subject: the cat, the boy = lomvelz, lamvoxs, possible answers: A, C.

The following word is in answer choice A, but not in the question sentence: black = roxalk. The correct answer is C.

7.21. Answer: A

Verb: to scare = upla, possible answers: A, D

Object: (the) neighbor = sosd, possible answers: A, D

Subject: (the) fire = poz, possible answers: A, D

Tense: present, possible answers: A, D

Others: Based on the existing examples, you can see that the subject is always at the beginning of the sentence. Answer: A

7.22. Answer: B

Verb: to listen to = slu, possible answers: A, B, D

Object: Music = telv, possible answers: A, B, D

Subject: (the) woman = zel, possible answers: B, D

Tense: present, possible answers: B, D

Others: (in the) kitchen = govt, possible answers: B, D; Based on the existing examples, you can see that the subject is always at the beginning of the sentence. Answer: B

APPENDIX: ANSWER SHEETS

Solving Quantitative Problems				
	A	B	C	D
1	☐	☐	☐	☐
2	☐	☐	☐	☐
3	☐	☐	☐	☐
4	☐	☐	☐	☐
5	☐	☐	☐	☐
6	☐	☐	☐	☐
7	☐	☐	☐	☐
8	☐	☐	☐	☐
9	☐	☐	☐	☐
10	☐	☐	☐	☐
11	☐	☐	☐	☐
12	☐	☐	☐	☐
13	☐	☐	☐	☐
14	☐	☐	☐	☐
15	☐	☐	☐	☐
16	☐	☐	☐	☐
17	☐	☐	☐	☐
18	☐	☐	☐	☐
19	☐	☐	☐	☐
20	☐	☐	☐	☐
21	☐	☐	☐	☐
22	☐	☐	☐	☐

Inferring Relationships				
	A	**B**	**C**	**D**
1	☐	☐	☐	☐
2	☐	☐	☐	☐
3	☐	☐	☐	☐
4	☐	☐	☐	☐
5	☐	☐	☐	☐
6	☐	☐	☐	☐
7	☐	☐	☐	☐
8	☐	☐	☐	☐
9	☐	☐	☐	☐
10	☐	☐	☐	☐
11	☐	☐	☐	☐
12	☐	☐	☐	☐
13	☐	☐	☐	☐
14	☐	☐	☐	☐
15	☐	☐	☐	☐
16	☐	☐	☐	☐
17	☐	☐	☐	☐
18	☐	☐	☐	☐
19	☐	☐	☐	☐
20	☐	☐	☐	☐
21	☐	☐	☐	☐
22	☐	☐	☐	☐

Completing Patterns

	A	B	C	D	E	F
1	☐	☐	☐	☐	☐	☐
2	☐	☐	☐	☐	☐	☐
3	☐	☐	☐	☐	☐	☐
4	☐	☐	☐	☐	☐	☐
5	☐	☐	☐	☐	☐	☐
6	☐	☐	☐	☐	☐	☐
7	☐	☐	☐	☐	☐	☐
8	☐	☐	☐	☐	☐	☐
9	☐	☐	☐	☐	☐	☐
10	☐	☐	☐	☐	☐	☐
11	☐	☐	☐	☐	☐	☐
12	☐	☐	☐	☐	☐	☐
13	☐	☐	☐	☐	☐	☐
14	☐	☐	☐	☐	☐	☐
15	☐	☐	☐	☐	☐	☐
16	☐	☐	☐	☐	☐	☐
17	☐	☐	☐	☐	☐	☐
18	☐	☐	☐	☐	☐	☐
19	☐	☐	☐	☐	☐	☐
20	☐	☐	☐	☐	☐	☐
21	☐	☐	☐	☐	☐	☐
22	☐	☐	☐	☐	☐	☐

Continuing Numerical Series

	-	0	1	2	3	4	5	6	7	8	9
01	☐	☐	☐	☐	☐	☐	☐	☐	☐	☐	☐
02	☐	☐	☐	☐	☐	☐	☐	☐	☐	☐	☐
03	☐	☐	☐	☐	☐	☐	☐	☐	☐	☐	☐
04	☐	☐	☐	☐	☐	☐	☐	☐	☐	☐	☐
05	☐	☐	☐	☐	☐	☐	☐	☐	☐	☐	☐
06	☐	☐	☐	☐	☐	☐	☐	☐	☐	☐	☐
07	☐	☐	☐	☐	☐	☐	☐	☐	☐	☐	☐
08	☐	☐	☐	☐	☐	☐	☐	☐	☐	☐	☐
09	☐	☐	☐	☐	☐	☐	☐	☐	☐	☐	☐
10	☐	☐	☐	☐	☐	☐	☐	☐	☐	☐	☐
11	☐	☐	☐	☐	☐	☐	☐	☐	☐	☐	☐
12	☐	☐	☐	☐	☐	☐	☐	☐	☐	☐	☐
13	☐	☐	☐	☐	☐	☐	☐	☐	☐	☐	☐
14	☐	☐	☐	☐	☐	☐	☐	☐	☐	☐	☐
15	☐	☐	☐	☐	☐	☐	☐	☐	☐	☐	☐
16	☐	☐	☐	☐	☐	☐	☐	☐	☐	☐	☐
17	☐	☐	☐	☐	☐	☐	☐	☐	☐	☐	☐
18	☐	☐	☐	☐	☐	☐	☐	☐	☐	☐	☐
19	☐	☐	☐	☐	☐	☐	☐	☐	☐	☐	☐
20	☐	☐	☐	☐	☐	☐	☐	☐	☐	☐	☐
21	☐	☐	☐	☐	☐	☐	☐	☐	☐	☐	☐
22	☐	☐	☐	☐	☐	☐	☐	☐	☐	☐	☐

Understanding and Interpreting Texts			
A	**B**	**C**	**D**
1 ☐	☐	☐	☐
2 ☐	☐	☐	☐
3 ☐	☐	☐	☐
4 ☐	☐	☐	☐
5 ☐	☐	☐	☐
6 ☐	☐	☐	☐
7 ☐	☐	☐	☐
8 ☐	☐	☐	☐
9 ☐	☐	☐	☐
10 ☐	☐	☐	☐
11 ☐	☐	☐	☐
12 ☐	☐	☐	☐
13 ☐	☐	☐	☐
14 ☐	☐	☐	☐
15 ☐	☐	☐	☐
16 ☐	☐	☐	☐
17 ☐	☐	☐	☐
18 ☐	☐	☐	☐
19 ☐	☐	☐	☐
20 ☐	☐	☐	☐
21 ☐	☐	☐	☐
22 ☐	☐	☐	☐

Using Representation Systems Flexibly				
	A	**B**	**C**	**D**
1	☐	☐	☐	☐
2	☐	☐	☐	☐
3	☐	☐	☐	☐
4	☐	☐	☐	☐
5	☐	☐	☐	☐
6	☐	☐	☐	☐
7	☐	☐	☐	☐
8	☐	☐	☐	☐
9	☐	☐	☐	☐
10	☐	☐	☐	☐
11	☐	☐	☐	☐
12	☐	☐	☐	☐
13	☐	☐	☐	☐
14	☐	☐	☐	☐
15	☐	☐	☐	☐
16	☐	☐	☐	☐
17	☐	☐	☐	☐
18	☐	☐	☐	☐
19	☐	☐	☐	☐
20	☐	☐	☐	☐
21	☐	☐	☐	☐
22	☐	☐	☐	☐

Recognizing Linguistic Structures			
A	**B**	**C**	**D**
1	☐	☐	☐	☐
2	☐	☐	☐	☐
3	☐	☐	☐	☐
4	☐	☐	☐	☐
5	☐	☐	☐	☐
6	☐	☐	☐	☐
7	☐	☐	☐	☐
8	☐	☐	☐	☐
9	☐	☐	☐	☐
10	☐	☐	☐	☐
11	☐	☐	☐	☐
12	☐	☐	☐	☐
13	☐	☐	☐	☐
14	☐	☐	☐	☐
15	☐	☐	☐	☐
16	☐	☐	☐	☐
17	☐	☐	☐	☐
18	☐	☐	☐	☐
19	☐	☐	☐	☐
20	☐	☐	☐	☐
21	☐	☐	☐	☐
22	☐	☐	☐	☐

EPILOGUE

Although we have reviewed the content several times to ensure its accuracy, mistakes can occur. Should you discover any errors, please do contact us. Apart from information about mistakes, we look forward to any feedback, praise, criticism or other comments you may have.

It is also worth checking out our homepage www.testasprep.com. Here, you can find more information about the TestAS as well as our ebooks in English and German.

We wish you all the best!

Your edulink team

OTHER BOOKS OF OUR PREPARATION SERIES FOR THE TESTAS

You can find our preparation series "Preparation for the TestAS Humanities, Cultural Studies and Social Sciences" on Amazon in print, and "Preparation for the TestAS Core Test" on www.testasprep.com as an ebook.

1. Preparation Book for the TestAS Humanities, Cultural Studies and Social Sciences: Understanding and Interpreting Texts & Using Representation Systems Flexibly

Content:

- Detailed explanation of the different types of text you will be given

- Explanation of the different types of questions and diagrams with numerous examples

- Two complete practice tests with 44 questions and detailed solutions

2. Preparation Book for the TestAS Humanities, Cultural Studies and Social Sciences: Recognizing Linguistic Structures

Content:

- Detailed explanations and solution strategies for translating the "languages" into English

- Explanation of the various rules of this section with numerous example questions

- Four practice tests for the section "Recognizing Linguistic Structures" with a total of 96 questions and detailed solutions

PRIVACY POLICY

The protection and security of your personal data is very important to us. Your personal data will not be used for advertising purposes or passed on to third parties. edulink GmbH only processes, notably stores, personal data of participants taking part in the contest for the duration and for the purpose of the implementation and handling of the competition. Your data will be processed on the basis of Art. 6 para. 1 (b) of the GDPR. edulink GmbH processes the following categories of personal data: name and contact data. The participant can exercise his or her right of objection at any time without giving reasons and revoke the declaration of consent given for the processing and storage of personal data. You can send the revocation to edulink GmbH either by post or by email. Furthermore, a right for disclosure, rectification, blocking and deletion of your personal data is in place. A transmission to a third country does not occur. Personal data will not be published. On request, we will send you a complete document in accordance with Art. 13 of the GDPR.

Legal information: The organizer of the competition is edulink GmbH (address: Schubertstr. 12, 80336 Munich, phone: +49 89 9975 6141, email: info@edu-link.de). Employees and family members of edulink GmbH are excluded from participation. Prizes will be distributed by the 15th of the following month. The end date of the competition is 31st January 2021. The winner will be notified by email. The voucher will be sent via email in digital form. A cash payment or transferability of the prize to other people is excluded. An exchange as well as warranties for defects regarding the profit are excluded. The winner will be announced without liability. A recourse to legal action is excluded.

End of the competition at any time: edulink GmbH can cancel or end the competition at any time without prior notice and without giving reasons. edulink GmbH can make use of this right in particular if it is no longer possible for the competition to be carried out properly due to technical or legal reasons.

Final provisions: A recourse to legal action is excluded. These conditions of participation as well as all resulting legal circumstances are subject exclusively to the law of the Federal Republic of Germany, unless another exclusive place of jurisdiction is required by law. Should individually provisions of these conditions of participation be or become invalid, the validity of the other conditions of participation remains unaffected.

Printed in Great Britain
by Amazon